The Rape of Lucrece

Thomas Heywood

TO THE READER.

It hath been no custom in me of all other men, courteous reader, to commit my Plays to the press; the reason though some may attribute to my own insufficiency,—I had rather subscribe in that to their severe censure, than by seeking to avoid the imputation of weakness, to incur greater suspicion of honesty; for though some have used a double sale of their labours, first to the stage, and after to the press, for my own part, I here proclaim myself ever faithful in the first, and never guilty of the last; yet since some of my Plays have, unknown to me, and without any of my direction, accidentally come into the printer's hands, and therefore so corrupt and mangled, copied only by the ear, that I have been as unable to know them, as ashamed to challenge them : this, therefore, I was the willinger to furnish out in his native habit; first being by consent; next, because the rest have been so wronged in being published in such savage and ragged ornaments. Accept it, courteous gentlemen, and prove as favorable readers as we have found you gracious auditors.

Your's,

T. H.

PERSONS REPRESENTED.

SERVIUS, *King of Rome.*
TARQUIN THE PROUD.
ARUNS,
SEXTUS, } *Sons of Tarquin.*
JUNIUS BRUTUS.
COLLATINE.
HORATIUS COCLES.
MUTIUS SCÆVOLA. } *Noble Romans.*
PUBLIUS VALERIUS.
LUCRETIUS.
PORSENNA, *King of the Tuscans.*
PORSENNA'S SECRETARY.
THE PRIEST OF APOLLO.
THE CLOWN.

TULLIA, *Wife of Tarquin.*
LUCRETIA, *Wife of Collatine.*
MIRABLE, *Lucretia's Maid.*

Senators, Sentinels, Servants, &c.

THE RAPE OF LUCRECE.

ACT I. SCENE I.

Enter TARQUIN THE PROUD, TULLIA, *and* ATTENDANTS.

Tul. WITHDRAW : we must have private conference
With our dear husband.   *[Attendants withdraw.*
 Tar. What would'st thou, wife ?
 Tul. Be what I am not; make thee greater far
Than thou can'st aim to be.
 Tar. Why, I am Tarquin.
 Tul. And I Tullia ; what of that ?
What diapasons more in Tarquin's name
Than in a subject's ? or what's Tullia
More in the sound than to become the name
Of a poor maid or waiting gentlewoman ?
I am a princess both by birth and thoughts,
Yet all's but Tullia : there's no resonance

In a bare style: my title bears no breadth,
Nor hath it any state   oh me, I'm sick!

   Tar. Sick, lady?

   Tul. Sick at heart.

   Tar. Why, my sweet Tullia?

   Tul. To be a queen I long; long, and am sick.
With ardency my hot appetite's a fire,
'Till my swoln fever be delivered
Of that great title—queen; my heart's all royal;
Not to be circumscrib'd in servile bounds.
While there's a king that rules the peers of Rome,
Tarquin makes legs, and Tullia curtsies low,
Bows at each nod, and must not near the state
Without obeisance; oh! I hate this awe;
My proud heart cannot brook it.

   Tar. Hear me, wife!

   Tul. I am no wife of Tarquin's, if not king.
Oh! had Jove made me man, I would have mounted
Above the base tribunals of the earth,
Up to the clouds, for pompous sovereignty.
Thou art a man; O bear my royal mind,
Mount heaven, and see if Tullia lag behind!
There is no earth in me; I am all fire:
Were Tarquin so, then should we both aspire.

   Tar. Oh, Tullia, though my body taste of dulness,
My soul is wing'd to soar as high as thine;
But note what flags our wings: forty-five years
The king, thy father, hath protected Rome.

   Tul. That makes for us: the people covet change;
E'en the best things in time grow tedious.

Tar. 'Twould seem unnatural in thee, my Tullia,
The reverend king, thy father, to depose.

Tul. A kingdom's quest makes sons and fathers foes.

Tar. And but by Servius' fall we cannot climb .
The balm that must anoint us is his blood.

Tul. Let's lave our brows, then, in that crimson flood ;
We must be bold and dreadless : who aspires,
Mounts by the lives of fathers, sons, and sires.

Tar. And so must I ; since, for a kingdom's love,
Thou can'st despise a father for a crown,
Tarquin shall mount, Servius be tumbled down,
For he usurps my state, and first depos'd
My father in my swathed infancy,
For which he shall be countant : to this end
I've sounded all the peers and senators ;
And, though unknown to thee, my Tullia,
They all embrace my faction ; and so they
Love change of state, a new king to obey.

Tul. Now is my Tarquin worthy Tullia's grace,
Since, in my arms, I thus a king embrace.

Tar. The king should meet this day in parliament,
With all the senate and estate of Rome;
His place will I assume, and there proclaim
All our decrees in royal Tarquin's name.   [*flourish.*

Enter SEXTUS, ARUNS, LUCRETIUS, VALERIUS, COLLATINE,
and SENATORS.

Luc. May it please thee, noble Tarquin, to attend
The king this day in the high Capitol ?

Tul. Attend?

Tar. We intend this day to see the Capitol.
You knew our father, good Lucretius?
   Luc. I did, my lord.
   Tar. Was not I his son?
The queen, my mother, was of royal thoughts
And pure heart, as unblemish'd innocence.
   Luc. What asks my lord?
   Tar. Sons should succeed their fathers; but anon
You shall hear more; high time that we were gone.
        [*flourish; exeunt all but Collatine and Valerius.*
   Col. There's moral sure in this, Valerius.
Here's model, yea, and matter too to breed
Strange meditations in the provident brains
Of our grave fathers; some strange project lives
This day in cradle that's but newly born.
   Val. No doubt, Collatine, no doubt; here's a giddy
and drunken world: it reels, it hath got the staggers;
the commonwealth is sick of an ague, of which nothing
can cure her but some violent and sudden affrightment.
   Col. The wife of Tarquin would be a queen; nay, of my
life, she is with child till she be so.
   Val. And longs to be brought to bed of a kingdom; I
divine, we shall see some scuffling to-day in the Capitol.
   Col. If there be any difference among the princes, and
senate, whose faction will Valerius follow?
   Val. Oh, Collatine, I am a true citizen; and in this I will
best shew myself to be one, to take part with the strongest.
If Servius o'ercome, I am liegeman to Servius, and if Tarquin subdue, I am for *vivat Tarquinius!*
   Col. Valerius, no more; this talk does but keep us from

the sight of this solemnity: by this the princes are en-
tering the Capitol: come! we must attend.   [*exeunt.*

SCENE II.

Enter TARQUIN, TULLIA, SEXTUS, ARUNS, *and* LUCRETIUS, *one
way:* BRUTUS *meeting them the other way, very humorously.*

Tar. This place is not for fools; this parliament
Assembles not the strains of idiotism,
Only the grave and wisest of the land :
Important are the affairs we have in hand.
Hence with that mome.

Luc. Brutus, forbear the presence.

Bru. Forbear the presence! why, pray?

Sex. None are admitted to this grave concourse
But wise men : nay, good Brutus.

Bru. You'll have an empty parliament then.

Aru. Here is no room for fools.

Bru. Then what mak'st thou here, or he, or he? oh Ju-
piter! if this command be kept strictly, we shall have empty
benches ; get you home you that are here, for here will be
nothing to do this day: a general concourse of wise men !
'twas never seen since the first chaos. Tarquin, if the general rule have no exceptions, thou wilt have an empty consistory.

Tul. Brutus, you trouble us.

Bru. How powerful am I, you Roman deities, that am
able to trouble her that troubles a whole empire? fools
exempted, and women admitted! laugh, Democritus! but
have you nothing to say to mad-men?

Tar. Madmen have here no place.

Bru. Then out of doors with Tarquin! what's he that may sit in a calm valley, and will chuse to repose on a tempestuous mountain, but a madman? that may live in tranquillous pleasures, and will seek out a kingdom's cares, but a madman? who would seek innovation in a commonwealth in public, or be over-rul'd by a curs'd wife in private, but a fool or a madman? Give me thy hand, Tarquin; shall we two be dismiss'd together from the Capitol?

Tar. Restrain his folly!

Tul. Drive the frantic hence!

Aru. Nay, Brutus.

Sex. Good Brutus.

Bru. Nay, soft, soft, good blood of the Tarquins, let's have a few cold words first, and I am gone in an instant: I claim the privilege of the nobility of Rome, and, by that privilege, my seat in the Capitol. I am a Lord by birth; my place is as free in the Capitol as, Horatius, thine, or thine, Lucretius, thine Sextus, Aruns thine, or any here: I am a Lord; an' you banish all the Lord fools from the presence, you'll have few to wait upon the king but gentlemen: [*they lay hands upon him.*] Nay, I am easily persuaded, then; hands off! since you will not have my company, you shall have my room.

[*aside.*] My room, indeed; for what I seem to be,
Brutus is not, but born great Rome to free.
The state is full of dropsy, and swollen big
With windy vapours, which my sword must pierce,
To purge th' infected blood, bred by the pride
Of these infected bloods. [*aloud.*] Nay, now I go;

Behold, I vanish, since 'tis Tarquin's mind :
One small fool goes, but great fools leaves behind.   [*exit*.
  Luc. 'Tis pity, one so gen'rously deriv'd
Should be depriv'd his best enduements thus,
And want the true directions of the soul.
  Tar. To leave these dilatory trifles, lords,
Now to the public business of the land.
Lords, take your several places.
  Luc. Not, great Tarquin, before the king assume his
      regal throne,
Whose coming we attend.
  Tul. He's come already.
  Luc. The king ?
  Tar. The king.
  Col. Servius ?
  Tar. Tarquinius.
  Luc. Servius is king.
  Tar. He was ; by power divine
The throne that long since he usurp'd is mine.
Here we enthrone ourselves ! cathedral state
Long since detain'd us, justly we resume :
Then let our friends and such as love us cry,
Live, Tarquin ! and enjoy this sovereignty !
  Omnes. Live, Tarquin ! and enjoy this sovereignty !
                        [*flourish*.

Enter VALERIUS.

  Val. The king himself, with such confederate peers
As stoutly embrace his faction, being inform'd
Of Tarquin's usurpation, armed comes,

Near to the entrance of the Capitol.

 Tar. No man give place; he that dares to rise
And do him reverence, we his love despise.

  Enter SERVIUS, HORATIUS, SCÆVOLA, *and* SOLDIERS.

 Ser. Traitor!
 Tar. Usurper!
 Ser. Descend.
 Tul. Sit still.
 Ser. In Servius' name, Rome's great imperial monarch,
I charge thee, Tarquin, disenthrone thyself,
And throw thee at our feet, prostrate for mercy.
 Hor. Spoke like a king.
 Tar. In Tarquin's name, now Rome's imperial monarch,
We charge thee, Servius, make free resignation
Of that arch'd wreath thou hast usurp'd so long.
 Tul. Words worth an empire.
 Hor. Shall this be brook'd, my sovereign?
Dismount the traitor.
 Sca. Touch him he that dares.
 Hor. Dares!
 Tul. Dares!
 Ser. Strumpet! no child of mine.
 Tul. Dotard! and not my father.
 Ser. Kneel to thy king.
 Tul. Submit thou to thy queen.
 Ser. Insufferable treason! with bright steel
Lop down these interponents that withstand
The passage to our throne.
 Hor. That Cocles dares.

Sex. We, with our steel, guard Tarquin and his chair.

Scæ. A Servius!   [*they fight—Servius is slain.*

Aru. A Tarquin!

Tar. Now are we king, indeed ! our awe is builded
Upon this royal base, the slaughtered body
Of a dead king : we by his ruin rise
To a monarchal throne.

Tul. We have our longing.
My father's death gives me a second life,
Much better than the first ; my birth was servile,
But this new breath of reign is large and free :
Welcome, my second life of sovereignty !

Luc. I have a daughter, but I hope of metal,
Subject to better temperature ; should my Lucrece
Be of this pride, these hands should sacrifice
Her blood unto the gods that dwell below ;
The abortive brat should not out-live my spleen ;
But Lucrece is my daughter, this my queen.   [*aside.*

Tul. Tear off the crown, that yet empales the temples
Of our usurping father : quickly, lords,
And in the face of his yet bleeding wounds,
Let us receive our honours.

Tar. The same breath
Gives our state life, that was th' usurper's death.

Tul. Here, then, by heaven's hand we invest ourselves :
Music, whose loftiest tones grace princes crown'd,
Unto our noble coronation sound.   [*flourish.*

VALERIUS *advances, with* HORATIUS *and* SCÆVOLA.

Tar. Whom doth Valerius to our state present ?

Val. Two valiant Romans ; this, Horatius Cocles,
This gentleman call'd Mutius Scævola ;
Who, whilst King Servius wore the diadem,
Upheld his sway and princedom by their loves.
But he being fall'n, since all the peers of Rome
Applaud King Tarquin in his sovereignty,
They with like suffrage greet your coronation.

Hor. This hand, allied unto the Roman crown,
Whom never fear dejected, or cast low,
Lays his victorious sword at Tarquin's feet,
And prostrates with that sword, allegiance.
King Servius' life we lov'd, but, he expir'd,
Great Tarquin's life is in our hearts desir'd.

Scæ. Who, whilst he rules with justice and integrity,
Shall with our dreadless hands our hearts command,
Even with the best employments of our lives ;
Since fortune lifts thee, we submit to fate ;
Ourselves are vassals to the Roman state.

Tar. Your rooms were empty in our train of friends,
Which we rejoice to see so well supplied :
Receive our grace, live in our clement favours,
In whose submission our young glory grows
To his ripe height : fall in our friendly train,
And strengthen with your loves our infant reign.

Hor. We live for Tarquin.

Scæ. And to thee alone, whilst justice keeps thy sword
and thou thy throne.

Tar. Then are you ours ; and now conduct us straight
In triumph through the populous streets of Rome,
To the king's palace our majestic seat ;

Your hearts, though freely proffer'd, we entreat.
  [*Sennet. As they march, Tullia treads on her father's*
       body and stays.

 Tul. What block is that we tread on?
 Luc. 'Tis the body
Of your deceased father; madam! queen!
Your shoe is crimson'd with his vital blood.   [*aside.*
 Tul. No matter, let his mangled body lie,
And with his base confederates strew the streets,
That, in disgrace of his usurped pride,
We o'er his trunk may in our chariot ride:
For, mounted like a queen, 'twould do me good
To wash my coach-naves in my father's blood.
 Luc. Here's a good child.   [*aside.*
 Tar. Remove it, we command,
And bear his carcase to the funeral pile,
Where, after this dejection, let it have
His solemn and due obsequies. Fair Tullia,
Thy hate to him grows from thy love to us;
Thou showest thyself in this unnatural strife
An unkind daughter, but a loving wife.
But on, unto our palace; this blest day,
A king's encrease grows by a king's decay.
        [*exeunt all but Brutus.*
 Bru. Murder the king! a high and capital treason.
Those giants that wag'd war against the gods,
For which th' o'erwhelmed mountains hurl'd by Jove
To scatter them, and give them timeless graves,
Was not more cruel than this butchery,
This slaughter made by Tarquin: but, the queen!

A woman, fie ! fie ! did not this she-parricide
Add to her father's wounds ? and when his body
Lay all besmear'd and stain'd in the blood royal,
Did not this monster, this infernal hag,
Make her unwilling charioteer drive on,
And with his shod wheels crush her father's bones ?
Break his craz'd scull, and dash his sparkled brains
Upon the pavements, whilst she held the reins ?
The affrighted sun at this abhorred object,
Put on a mask of blood, and yet she blush'd not.
Jove, art thou just ? hast thou reward for piety,
And for offence no vengeance ? or cans't punish
Felons, and pardon traitors ? chastise murderers,
And wink at parricides ? if thou be worthy,
As well we know thou art, to fill the throne
Of all eternity, then with that hand
That flings the trifulk thunder, let the pride
Of these our irreligious monarchisers
Be crown'd in blood.   This makes poor Brutus mad,
To see sin frolic, and the virtuous sad.

Enter SEXTUS and ARUNS.

Aru. Soft ! here's Brutus ; let us acquaint him with the
      news.
Sex. Content :—now, cousin Brutus.
Bru. Who, I, your kinsman ? though I be of the blood of
the Tarquins, yet no cousin, gentle prince.
Aru. And why so, Brutus, scorn you our alliance ?
Bru. No, I was cousin to the Tarquins, when they were
subjects, but dare claim no kindred as they are sovereigns:

Brutus is not so mad, though he be merry; but he hath wit enough to keep his head on his shoulders.

Aru. Why do you, lord, thus lose your hours, and neither profess war nor domestic profit? The first might beget you love, the other riches.

Bru. Because I would live; have I not answered you,—'cause I would live: fools and mad men are no rubs in the way of usurpers; the firmament can brook but one sun, and for my part I must not shine: I had rather live an obscure black, than appear a fair white to be shot at; the end of all is, I would live. Had Servius been a shrub, the wind had not shook him; or a mad-man, he'd not perished: I covet no more wit nor employment than as much as will keep life and soul together: I would but live.

Aru. You are satirical, cousin Brutus; but, to the purpose: the king dreamt a strange and ominous dream last night, and, to be resolv'd of the event, my brother Sextus and I must to the Oracle.

Sex. And because we would be well accompanied, we have got leave of the king that you, Brutus, shall associate us, for our purpose is to make a merry journey on't.

Bru. So you'd carry me along with you, to be your fool, and make you merry.

Sex. Not our fool, but—

Bru. To make you merry: I shall, nay, I will make you merry, or tickle you till you laugh! The Oracle! I'll go to be resolv'd of some doubts private to myself: nay, Princes, I am so much endear'd both to your loves and companies, that you shall not have the power to be rid of me. What limits have we for our journey?

Sex. Five days, no more.

Bru. I shall fit me to your preparations : but one thing more; goes Collatine along ?

Sex. Collatine is troubl'd with the common disease of all new married men; he's sick of the wife : his excuse is, forsooth, that Lucrece will not let him go; but you, having neither wife nor wit to hold you, I hope will not disappoint us.

Bru. Had I both, yet should you prevail with me above either.

Aru. We shall expect you.

Bru. Horatius Cocles and Mutius Scævola are not engag'd in this expedition ?

Aru. No, they attend the King : farewell.

Bru. Lucretius stays at home too, and Valerius ?

Sex. The palace cannot spare them.

Bru. None but we three ?

Sex. We three.

Bru. We three; well, five days' hence.

Sex. You have the time, farewell.

[exeunt Sextus and Aruns.

Bru. The time, I hope, cannot be circumscrib'd
Within so short a limit; Rome and I
Are not so happy; what's the reason, then,
Heaven spares his rod so long ? Mercury, tell me !
I hav't, the fruit of pride is yet but green,
Not mellow; though it grows apace, it comes not
To his full height : Jove oft delays his vengeance,
That when it haps 't may prove more terrible.
Despair not, Brutus, then, but let thy country

And thee take this last comfort after all,
Pride, when thy fruit is ripe, 'tmust rot, and fall!
But, to the Oracle.   [*exit*.

SCENE III.

Enter HORATIUS *and* SCÆVOLA.

Hor. I would I were no Roman.
Scæ. Cocles, why?
Hor. I am discontented, and dare not speak my thoughts.
Scæ. What! shall I speak them for you?
Hor. Mutius, do.
Scæ. Tarquin is proud.
Hor. Thou hast them.
Scæ. Tyrannous.
Hor. True.
Scæ. Insufferably lofty.
Hor. Thou hast hit me.
Scæ. And shall I tell thee what I prophesy
Of his succeeding rule?
   Hor. No, I'll do't for thee; Tarquin's ability will, in the
       weal,
Beget a weak unable impotence;
His strength make Rome and our dominions weak;
His soaring high make us to flag our wings,
And fly close by the earth; his golden feathers
Are of such vastness, that they spread like sails,
And so becalm us, that we have not air
Able to raise our plumes, to taste the pleasures of our own
       elements.

Sca. We are one heart, our thoughts and our desires are
suitable.

Hor. Since he was king he bears him like a god :
His wife, like Pallas, or the wife of Jove,
Will not be spoke to without sacrifice,
And homage sole due to the deities.

Enter LUCRETIUS.

Sca. What haste with good Lucretius ?
Luc. Haste, but small speed :
I had an earnest suit unto the king,
About some business that concerns the weal
Of Rome and us ; 'twill not be listen'd to :
He has took upon him such ambitious state,
That he abandons conference with his peers;
Or if he chance to endure our tongues so much,
As but to hear their sonance, he despises
The intent of all our speeches, our advices,
And counsel ; thinking his own judgment only
To be approv'd in matters military ;
And in affairs domestic we are but mutes,
And fellows of no parts, viols unstrung,
Our notes too harsh to strike in princes' ears.
Great Jove amend it !
   Hor. Whither will you, my lord?
   Luc. No matter where, if from the court.   I'll home to
         Collatine
And to my daughter, Lucrece : home breeds safety ;
Danger's begot in court ; a life retir'd
Must please me now perforce : then, noble Scævola,

And you, my dear Horatius, farewell both :
Where industry is scorn'd, let's welcome sloth.

Enter COLLATINE.

Hor. Nay, good Lucretius, do not leave us thus :
See, here comes Collatine; but where's Valerius ?
How does he taste these times ?

Col. Not giddily, like Brutus; nor passionately,
Like old Lucretius, with his tear-swoln eyes ;
Not laughingly, like Mutius Scævola ;
Nor bluntly, like Horatius Cocles here ;
He has usurp'd a stranger garb of humour,
Distinct from these in nature every way.

Luc. How is he relish'd? can his eyes forbear,
In this strange state, to shed a passionate tear ?

Scæ. Can he forbear to laugh with Scævola,
At that which passionate weeping cannot mend ?

Hor. Nay, can his thought shape ought but melancholy,
To see these dang'rous passages of state ?
How is he temper'd, noble Collatine ?

Col. Strangely; he is all song, he's ditty all ;
Note that : Valerius hath given up the court,
And wean'd himself from the king's consistory,
In which his sweet harmonious tongue grew harsh ;
Whether it be that he is discontent,
Yet would not so appear before the king,
Or whether in applause of these new edicts,
Which so distaste the people, or what cause
I know not, but now he's all musical.
Unto the council-chamber he goes singing ;

And whilst the king his wilful edicts makes,
In which none's tongue is powerful save the king's,
He's in a corner relishing strange airs.
Conclusively, he's from a toward hopeful gentleman,
Transhap'd to a mere ballader; none knowing
Whence should proceed this transmutation.

Enter VALERIUS.

Hor. See, where he comes.   Morrow, Valerius!
Luc. Morrow, my lord!

Song—VALERIUS.

When Tarquin first in court began,
And was approved king,
Some men for sudden joy 'gan weep,
But I for sorrow sing.

Scæ. Ha, ha! how long has my Valerius
Put on this strain of mirth, or what's the cause?

Song—VALERIUS.

Let humour change and spare not,
Since Tarquin's proud, I care not;
His fair words so bewitch'd my delight,
That I doted on his sight.
Now he is chang'd, cruel thoughts embracing,
And my deserts disgracing.

Hor. Upon my life, he's either mad or love-sick.
Oh, can Valerius, but so late a statesman,
Of whom the public weal deserv'd so well,
Tune out his age in songs and canzonets,

Whose voice should thunder counsel in the ears
Of Tarquin and proud Tullia? Think, Valerius,
What that proud woman, Tullia, is; 'twill put thee
Quite out of tune.

Song—VALERIUS.

> Now what is love I will thee tell,
> It is the fountain and the well,
> Where pleasure and repentance dwell:
> It is perhaps the *sansing bell,
> That rings all in to heaven or hell,
> And this is love, and this is love, as I hear tell.
>
> Now what is love I will you show:
> A thing that creeps and cannot go;
> A prize that passeth to and fro;
> A thing for me, a thing for mo';
> And he that proves shall find it so,
> And this is love, and this is love, sweet friend, I trow.

Luc. Valerius, I shall quickly change thy cheer,
And make thy passionate eyes lament with mine:
Think how that worthy prince, our kinsman king,
Was butcher'd in the marble Capitol!
Shall Servius Tullius unregarded die
Alone of thee, whom all the Roman ladies,
Even yet with tear-swoln eyes, and sorrowful souls,
Compassionate, as well he merited?
To these lamenting dames what canst thou sing,
Whose griefs through all the Roman temples ring?

---

* *Sance bell*—Saints' bell, or the *Sanctus* bell, a small bell which called to prayers and other holy offices.

Song—VALERIUS.

Lament, ladies, lament,
Lament the Roman land,
The king is fra thee hent,
Was doughty on his hand.
We'll gang into the Kirk,
His dead corpse we'll embrace,
And when we see him dead,
We aye will cry, alas!   Fa la, lero la.
Tara rara roune ta re, &c.

Hor. This music mads me, I all mirth despise.
Luc. To hear him sing draws rivers from mine eyes.
Scæ. It pleaseth me; for since the court is harsh,
And looks askance on soldiers, let's be merry,
Court ladies, sing, drink, dance, and every man
Get him a mistress, coach it in the country,
And taste the sweets of it; what thinks Valerius
Of Scævola's last counsel?

Song—VALERIUS.

Why since we soldiers cannot prove,
  And grief it is to us therefore,
Let every man get him a love,
  To trim her well, and fight no more.
  That we may taste of lovers' bliss;
  Be merry and blithe, embrace and kiss,
  That ladies may say, some more of this,
  That ladies may say, some more of this.

Since court and city both grow proud,
  And safety you delight to hear,

We in the country will us shroud,
    Where lives to please both eye and ear ;
    The nightingale sings jug, jug, jug,
    The little lamb leaps after his dug,
    And the pretty milk-maids they look so smug,
    And the pretty milk-maids, &c.

Come, Scævola, shall we go and be idle ?
  Luc. I'll in to weep.
  Hor. But I my gall to grate.
  Scæ. I'll laugh at time, till it will change our fate.
                        [exeunt all but Collatine.
  Col. Thou art not what thou seem'st, Lord Scævola ;
Thy heart mourns in thee, though thy visage smile :
And so does thy soul weep, Valerius,
Although thy habit sing : for these new humours
Are but put on for safety, and to arm them
Against the pride of Tarquin, from whose danger,
None great in love, in counsel, or opinion,
Can be kept safe : this makes me lose my hours
At home with Lucrece, and abandon court.

Enter CLOWN.

  Clown. Fortune, I embrace thee, that thou hast assisted me in finding my master ! The gods of good Rome keep my lord and master out of all bad company !
  Col. Sirrah, the news with you.
  Clown. Would you ha' court news, camp news, city news, or country news ? or would you know what's the news at home ?

Col. Let me know all the news.

Clown. The news at court is, that a small leg and a silk stocking is in the fashion for your lord ; and the water that god Mercury makes is in request with your lady.   The heaviness of the king's wine makes many a light head, and the emptiness of his dishes many full bellies ; eating and drinking was never more in use : you shall find the baddest legs in boots, and the worst faces in masks.   They keep their old stomachs still ; the king's good cook had the most wrong ; for that which was wont to be private only to him, is now usurp'd among all the other officers : for now every man in his place, to the prejudice of the master cook, makes bold to lick his own fingers.

Col. The news in the camp ?

Clown. The greatest news in the camp is, that there is no news at all ; for being no camp at all, how can there be any tidings from it ?

Col. Then, for the city ?

Clown. The senators are rich, their wives fair, credit grows cheap, and traffic dear ; for you have many that are broke ; the poorest man that is may take up what he will, so he will be but bound to a post till he pay the debt. There was one courtier lay with twelve men's wives in the suburbs, and pressing farther to make one more cuckold within the walls, and being taken with the manner, had nothing to say for himself, but this, he that made twelve made thirteen.

Col. Now, sir, for the country ?

Clown. There is no news there but at the ale-house, there's the most receipt ; and is it not strange, my lord, that so many men love ale that know not what ale is ?

Col. Why, what is ale?

Clown. Why, ale is a kind of juice, made of the precious grain called malt; and what is malt? malt's M, A, L, T; and what is M, A, L, T? M much, A ale, L little, T thrift; that is, much ale, little thrift.

Col. Only the news at home and I have done.

Clown. My lady must needs speak with you about earnest business, that concerns her nearly, and I was sent in all haste to entreat your lordship to come away.

Col. And could'st thou not have told me? Lucrece stay, And I stand trifling here!   Follow, away!

Clown. Aye, marry, sir, the way into her were a way worth following; and that's the reason that so many serving-men, that are familiar with their mistresses, have lost the name of servitors, and are now called their masters' followers.   Rest you merry!   [*exeunt.*

ACT II. SCENE I.

Enter APOLLO'S PRIESTS, *with tapers; after them,* ARUNS, SEXTUS, *and* BRUTUS, *with their oblations, all kneeling before the Oracle.   Music.*

> *Priest.* O, thou Delphian god, inspire
> Thy priests, and, with celestial fire
> Shot from thy beams, crown our desire,
>   That we may follow,
>
> In these thy true and hallow'd measures,
> The utmost of thy heavenly treasures,
> According to the thoughts and pleasures
>   Of great Apollo.

Our hearts with inflammations burn,
Great Tarquin and his people mourn,
'Till from thy temple we return
                    With some glad tiding.

Then tell us, shall great Rome be blest,
And róyal Tarquin live in rest,
That gives his high-ennobled breast
                    To thy safe guiding ?

Orac. Then Rome her ancient honours wins,
When she is purg'd from Tullia's sins.
Bru. Gramercies, Phœbus, for these spells ;
Phœbus alone, alone excels.
Sex. Tullia, perhaps, sinn'd in our grandsire's death,
And hath not yet by reconcilement made
Atone with Phœbus, at whose shrine we kneel :
Yet, gentle priest, let us thus far prevail,
To know if Tarquin's seed shall govern Rome,
And, by succession, claim the royal wreath ?
Behold me, younger of the Tarquin's race ;
This elder, Aruns, both the sons of Tullia ;
This, Junius Brutus, though a mad-man, yet
Of the high blood of the Tarquins.
Priest. Sextus, peace !

Tell us, O thou that shin'st so bright,
From whom the world receives his light,
Whose absence is perpetual night,
                    Whose praises ring :

Is it with heaven's applause decreed,
When Tarquin's soul from earth is freed,

That noble Sextus shall succeed
                              In Rome as King?

Bru. Aye, Oracle, hast thou lost thy tongue?
Aru. Tempt him again, fair priest.
Sex. If not as king, let Delphian Phœbus yet
Thus much resolve us : who shall govern Rome,
Or, of us three, bear great'st pre-eminence?
Priest. Sextus, I will ;

    Yet, sacred Phœbus, we entreat,
    Which of these three shall be great,
    With largest power and state replete,
              By the heavens' doom?

    Phœbus, thy thoughts no longer smother.
    Orac. He that first shall kiss his mother,
    Shall be powerful, and no other,
             Of you three in Rome.

Sex. Shall kiss his mother!   [*Brutus falls.*
Bru. Mother Earth, to thee an humble kiss I tender.
                                          [*aside.*

Aru. What means Brutus?
Bru. The blood of the slaughter'd sacrifice made this
floor as slippery as the place where Tarquin treads;
'tis glassy and as smooth as ice: I was proud to hear
the Oracle so gracious to the blood of the Tarquins, and
so I fell.
Sex. Nothing but so, then to the Oracle.
I charge thee Aruns, Junius Brutus, thee,
To keep the sacred doom of th' Oracle
From all our train ; lest when the younger lad,

Our brother, now at home, sits dandled
Upon fair Tullia's lap, this understanding,
May kiss our beauteous mother, and succeed.

Aru. Let the charge go round ;—
It shall go hard but I'll prevent you, Sextus.   [*aside.*

Sex. I fear not the madman, Brutus; and for Aruns, let
me alone to buckle with him : I'll be the first at my mother's lips for a kingdom.

Bru. If the madman have not been before you, Sextus.
If oracles be oracles, their phrases are mystical; they
speak still in clouds: had he meant a natural mother, he
would not have spoke it by circumstance.   [*aside.*

Sex. Tullia, if ever thy lips were pleasing to me, let it
be at my return from the Oracle.

Aru. If a kiss will make me a king, Tullia, I will spring
to thee, though through the blood of Sextus.   [*aside.*

Bru. Earth, I acknowledge no mother but thee ; accept
me as thy son, and I shall shine as bright in Rome as
Apollo himself in his temple at Delphos.

Sex. Our superstition's ended, sacred priest,
Since we have had free answer from the gods,
To whose fair altars we have done due right,
And hallowed them with presents acceptable.
Let's now return, treading these holy measures,
With which we enter'd great Apollo's temple.
Now, Phœbus, let thy sweet tun'd organs sound,
Whose sphere—like music, must direct our feet
Upon the marble pavement : after this,
We'll gain a kingdom by a mother's kiss.   [*exeunt.*

SCENE II.

A table and chairs prepared; TARQUIN, TULLIA, COLLATINE,
SCÆVOLA, HORATIUS, LUCRETIUS, VALERIUS, LORDS.

Tar. Attend us with your persons, but your ears
Be deaf unto our counsels.
           [*The Lords fall off on either aside and attend.*
Tul. Farther yet.
Tar. Now, Tullia, what must be concluded next?
Tul. The kingdom you have got by policy
You must maintain by pride.
Tar. Good.
Tul. Those that were late of the king's faction
Cut off for fear they prove rebellious.
Tar. Better.
Tul. Since you gain nothing by the popular love,
Maintain by fear your princedom.
Tar. Excellent; thou art our oracle, and, save from thee,
We will admit no counsel: we obtain'd
Our state by cunning; it must be kept by strength:
And such as cannot love, we'll teach to fear;
T' encourage which, upon our better judgment,
And to strike greater terror to the world,
I have forbid thy father's funeral.
Tul. No matter.
Tar. All capital causes are by us discuss'd,
Travers'd, and executed, without counsel;
We challenge too, by our prerogative,

The goods of such as strive against our state ;
The freest citizens, without attaint,
Arraign, or judgment, we to exile doom.
The poorer are our drudges, rich our prey,
And such as dare not strive our rule obey.

   Tul. Kings are as gods, and divine sceptres bear,
The gods command, for mortal tribute, fear;
But, royal lord, we that despise their love,
Must seek some means how to maintain this awe.

   Tar. By foreign leagues, and by our strength abroad.
Shall we that are decreed above our people,
Whom heaven hath made our vassals, reign with them ?
No ; kings, above the rest tribunal'd high,
Should with no meaner than with kings ally:
For this, we to Mamilius Tusculan,
The Latin king, have given in marriage
Our royal daughter. now his people's ours,
The neighbour princes are subdu'd by arms :
And whom we could not conquer by constraint,
Them we have sought to win by courtesy;
Kings that are proud, yet would secure their own,
By love abroad shall purchase fear at home.

   Tul. We are secure ; and yet our greatest strength
Is in our children; how dare treason look
Us in the face having issue ? Barren princes
Breed danger in their singularity;
Having none to succeed, their claim dies in them.

   Tar. Tullia's wise and apprehensive ; were our princely
        sons,
Sextus and Aruns, back returned safe,

With an applausive answer of the gods
From th' Oracle, our state were able then,
Being gods ourselves, to scorn the hate of men.

Enter SEXTUS, ARUNS, *and* BRUTUS.

Sex. Where's Tullia?
Aru. Where's our mother?
Hor. Yonder, princes, at council with the king.
Tul. Our sons return'd!
Sex. Royal mother!
Aru. Renowned queen!
Sex. I love her best, therefore will Sextus do his duty
    first.
Aru. Being eldest in my birth, I'll not be youngest
In zeal to Tullia.
Bru. To't, lads.
Aru. Mother, a kiss.
Sex. Though last in birth, let me be first in love.
A kiss, fair mother.
Aru. Shall I lose my right?
Sex. Aruns shall down, were Aruns twice my brother,
If he presumes 'fore me to kiss my mother.
Aru. Aye, Sextus, think this kiss to be a crown, thus
    would we tug for't.   [*they struggle.*
Sex. Aruns, thou must down.
Tar. Restrain them, lords.
Bru. Nay, to't, boys; O 'tis brave! they tug for shadows,
I the substance have.   [*aside.*
Aru. Through armed gates and thousand swords I'll
    break

To shew my duty; let my valour speak.

     [breaks from the Lords, and kisses her.

 Sex. O, heavens! you have dissolv'd me.

 Aru. Here I stand,

What I have done to answer with this hand.

 Sex. O, all ye Delphian gods, look down and see

How for these wrongs I will revenged be.

 Tar. Curb in the proud boy's fury; let us know

From whence this discord riseth.

 Tul. From our love; how happy are we in our issue

   now!

When as our sons, even with their bloods, contend

T' exceed in duty; we accept your zeal.

This, your superlative degree of kindness,

So much prevails with us, that to the king

We engage our own dear love 'twixt his incensement

And your presumption; you are pardoned both.

And, Sextus, though you fail'd in your first proffer,

We do not yet esteem you least in love; ascend, and touch

   our lips.

 Sex. Thank you, no.

 Tul. Then to thy knee we will descend thus low.

 Sex. Nay, now it shall not need: how great's my heart!

 Aru. In Tarquin's crown thou now hast lost thy part.

 Sex. No kissing now, Tarquin; great queen, adieu!

Aruns, on earth we have no foe but you.

 Tar. What means this their unnatural enmity?

 Tul. Hate, born from love.

 Tar. Resolve us then, how did the gods accept

Our sacrifice? how are they pleas'd with us?

How long will they applaud our sovereignty?

Bru. Shall I tell the king?

Tar. Do, cousin, with the process of your journey,

Bru. I will.—We went from hither, when we went from hence, arrived thither when we landed there; made an end of our prayers when we had done our orisons, when thus quoth Phœbus,—"Tarquin shall be happy whilst he is blest, govern while he reigns, wake when he sleeps not, sleep when he wakes not, quaff when he drinks, feed when he eats, gape when his mouth opens, live till he die, and die when he can live no lónger."—So Phœbus commends him to you.

Tar. Mad Brutus still! Son Aruns, what say you?

Aru. That the great gods to whom the potent king
Of this large empire sacrific'd by us,
Applaud your reign, commend your sovereignty:
And, by a general synod, grant to Tarquin
Long days, fair hopes, majestic government.

Bru. Adding withal, that to depose the late king, which, in others, had been high treason, in Tarquin was honour: what in Brutus had been usurpation, in Tarquin was lawful succession: and for Tullia, though it be parricide for a child to kill her father, in Tullia it was charity, by death to rid him of all his calamities. Phœbus himself said she was a good child, and shall not I say as he says, to tread upon her father's skull,
Sparkle his brains upon her chariot wheel,
And wear the sacred tincture of his blood
Upon her servile shoe? but more than this,
After his death deny him the due claim
Of all mortality, a funeral,

D

An earthen sepulchre, this, this, quoth the oracle,
Save Tullia, none would do.

   Tul. Brutus, no more; least with the eyes of wrath and
        incens'd fury,
We look into thy humour: were not madness
And folly to thy words a privilege,
Even in thy last reproof of our proceedings
Thou had'st pronounc'd thy death.

   Bru. If Tullia will send Brutus abroad for news, and after, at his return, not endure the telling of it; let Tullia
either get closer ears, or get for Brutus a stricter tongue.

   Tul. How, sir?

   Bru. God be wi' ye!   [*exit.*

   Tar. Alas! 'tis madness, pardon him, not spleen;
Nor is it hate, but frenzy. We are pleas'd
To hear the gods propitious to our prayers.
But whither 's Sextus gone? resolve us, Cocles;
We saw thee in his parting follow him.

   Hor. I heard him say, he would straight take his
        horse,
And to the warlike Gabines, enemies to Rome, and you.

   Tar. Save them we have no opposites.
Dares the proud boy confederate with our foes?
Attend us, lords; we must new battles wage,
And with bright arms confront the proud boy's rage.
      [*exeunt all but Lucretius, Collatine, Horatius, Va-*
        lerius, and Scævola.

   Hor. Had I as many souls as drops of blood
In these branch'd veins, as many lives as stars
Stuck in yon azure roof, and were to die

More deaths than I have wasted weary minutes
To grow to this, I'd hazard all, and more,
To purchase freedom to thus bondag'd Rome.
I'm vex'd to see this virgin conqueress
Wear shackles in my sight.

   Luc. Oh! would my tears
Would rid great Rome of these prodigious fears!

Enter BRUTUS.

   Bru. What, weeping-ripe, Lucretius? possible? now lords, lads, friends, fellows, young madcaps, gallants, and old courtly ruffians, all subjects under one tyranny and therefore should be partners of one and the same unanimity! Shall we go single ourselves by two and two, and go talk treason? then 'tis but his yea, and my nay, if we be call'd to question: or shall's go use some violent bustling to break through this thorny servitude: or shall we every man go sit like a man in desperation, and with Lucretius weep at Rome's misery? now am I for all things, any thing, or nothing: I can laugh with Scævola, weep with this good old man, sing *oh hone, hone*, with Valerius, fret with Horatius Cocles, be mad like myself, or neutrize with Collatine. Say, what shall's do?

   Hor. Fret.

   Val. Sing.

   Luc. Weep.

   Scæ. Laugh.

   Bru. Rather let's all be mad
That Tarquin he still reigneth, Rome's still sad.

   Col. You are madmen all that yield so much to passion.

You lay yourselves too open to your enemies;
That would be glad to pry into your deeds,
And catch advantage to ensnare our lives.
The king's fear, like a shadow, dogs you still,
Nor can you walk without it: I commend
Valerius most, and noble Scævola,
That what they cannot mend, seem not to mind.
By my consent let's all wear out our hours
In harmless sports: hawk, hunt, game, sing, drink, dance,
So shall we seem offenceless, and live safe
In danger's bloody jaws; where, being humorous,
Cloudy and curiously inquisitive
Into the king's proceedings, there arm'd fear
May search into us, call our deeds to question,
And so prevent all future expectation
Of wish'd amendment; let us stay the time
Till heaven have made them ripe for just revenge,
When opportunity is offer'd us,
And then strike home; till then, do what you please.
No discontented thought my mind shall seize.

Bru. I am of Collatine's mind now. Valerius, sing us a bawdy song, and make us merry: nay it shall be so.

Val. Brutus shall pardon me.

Scæ. The time that should have been seriously spent in the State-house, I have learnt securely to spend in a wenching house, and now I profess myself any thing but a statesman.

Hor. The more thy vanity.

Luc. The less thy honour.

Val. The more his safety, and the less his fear.

Song.—Valerius.

She that denies me, I would have ;
Who craves me, I despise.
  Venus hath power to rule mine heart,
But not to please mine eyes.
  Temptatious offer'd, I still scorn ;
Deny'd; I cling them still,
  I'll neither glut mine appetite,
Nor seek to starve my will.
  Diana, double-cloth'd, offends ;
So Venus, naked quite ;
  The last begets a surfeit, and
The other no delight.
  That crafty girl shall please me best
That no for yea can say,
  And every wanton willing kiss
Can season with a nay.

Bru. We have been mad lords long, now let us be merry lords. Horatius, maugre thy melancholy, and, Lucretius, in spite of thy sorrow, I'll have a song ; a subject for the ditty.

Hor. Great Tarquin's pride, and Tullia's cruelty.

Bru. Dangerous ; no.

Luc. The tyrannies of the court, and vassalage of the city.

Sca. Neither ; shall I give the subject ?

Bru. Do, and let it be of all the pretty wenches in Rome.

Sca. It shall, it shall ;—shall it, Valerius ?

Val. Any thing according to my poor acquaintance and little conversance.

Bru. Nay, you shall stay, Horatius; Lucretius, so shall you. He removes himself from the love of Brutus, that shrinks my side till we have had a song of all the pretty suburbians : sit round ; when, Valerius ?

Song.—VALERIUS.

Shall I woo the lovely Molly ?
She's so fair, so fat, so jolly,
But she has a trick of folly,
Therefore I'll have none of Molly. No, no, no, no,
      no, no.
I'll have none of Molly, no, no, no.
Oh, the cherry lips of Nelly,
They are red and soft as jelly,
But too well she loves her belly,
Therefore I'll have none of Nelly. No, no, no, &c.
What say you to bonny Betty,
Have you seen a lass so pretty ?
But her body is so sweaty,
Therefore I'll have none of Betty. No, no, no, &c.
When I dally with my Dolly,
She is full of melancholy,
Oh, that wench is pestilent holy,
Therefore I'll have none of Dolly. No, no, no, &c.
I could fancy lovely Nanny,
But she has the loves of many,
Yet herself she loves not any,
Therefore I'll have none of Nanny.   No, no, &c.
In a flax shop I spy'd Rachel,
Where she her flax and tow did hatchel,*

* To *hatchel*—to dress flax, hemp, &c.

> But her cheeks hang like a satchel,
> Therefore I'll have none of Rachel. No, no, &c.
> In a corner I met Biddy,
> Her heels were light, her head was giddy,
> She fell down and somewhat did I,
> Therefore I'll have none of Biddy.   No, no, &c.

Bru. The rest we'll hear within. What offence is there in this, Lucretius? what hurt's in this, Horatius? Is it not better to sing with our heads on, than to bleed with our heads off?   I ne'er took Collatine for a politician till now. Come, Valerius, we'll run over all the wenches of Rome, from the community of lascivious Flora to the chastity of divine Lucrece: come, good Horatius.   [*exeunt.*

ACT III. SCENE I.

Enter LUCRECE, MAID, *and* CLOWN.

Luc. A chair !

Clown. A chair for my lady, Mistress Mirable, do you not hear my lady call.

Luc. Come near, sir; be less officious
In duty, and use more attention :
Nay, gentlewoman, we exempt not you
From our discourse; you must afford an ear,
As well as he, to what we have to say.

Maid. I still remain your hand-maid.

Luc. Sirrah, I have seen you oft familiar
With this my maid and waiting gentlewoman,

As casting amorous glances, wanton looks,
And privy becks savouring incontinence;
I let you know you are not for my service
Unless you grow more civil.

Clown. Indeed, madam, for my own part I wish Mistress Mirable well, as one fellow servant ought to wish to another; but to say as that ever I flung any sheeps' eyes in her face,—how say you, Mistress Mirable, did I ever offer it?

Luc. Nay, mistress, I have seen you answer him
With gracious looks, and some uncivil smiles,
Retorting eyes, and giving his demeanor
Such welcome as becomes not modesty.
Know henceforth there shall no lascivious phrase,
Suspicious look, or shadow of incontinence,
Be entertain'd by any that attend on Roman Lucrece.

Maid. Madam, I?

Luc. Excuse it not, for my premeditate thought
Speaks nothing out of rashness, nor vain hearsay,
But what my own experience testifies
Against you both; let then this mild reproof
Forewarn you of the like; my reputation,
Which is held precious in the eyes of Rome,
Shall be no shelter to the least intent
Of looseness; leave all familiarity,
And quite renounce acquaintance,
Or I here discharge you both my service.

Clown. For my own part, madam, as I am a true Roman by nature, though no Roman by my nose, I never spent the least lip-labour on Mistress Mirable, never so much as glanced, never used any winking or pinking, never nodded at her, no, not so much as when I was asleep, never asked her the question so much as what's her name : if you bring any man, woman, or child that can say so much behind my back, as for he did but kiss her ; for I did but kiss her and so let her go ; let my Lord Collatine, instead of plucking my coat, pluck my skin over my ears and turn me away naked, that, wheresoever I shall come, I may be held a raw serving man hereafter.

Luc. Sirrah, you know our mind.

Clown. If ever I knew what belongs to these cases, or yet know what they mean ; if ever I us'd any plain dealing, or were ever worth such a jewel, would I might die like a beggar ; if ever I were so far read in my grammar, as to know what an interjection is, or a conjunction copulative, would I might never have good of my *qui, quæ, quod :* why, do you think, madam, I have no more care of myself, being but a stripling, than to go to it at these years? flesh and blood cannot endure it ; I shall even spoil one of the best faces in Rome with crying at your unkindness.

Luc. I have done : see, if you can spy your lord returning from the court, and give me notice what strangers he brings home with him.

Enter COLLATINE, VALERIUS, HORATIUS, *and* SCÆVOLA.

Clown. Yes, I'll go ; but see, kind man, he saves me a labour.

Hor. Come, Valerius, let's hear in our way to the house of Collatine, that saying you went late hammering of, concerning the taverns in Rome.

Val. Only this, Horatius.

Song.—VALERIUS.

The gentry to the King's Head,
The nobles to the Crown,
The knights unto the Golden Fleece,
And to the Plough the clown.
The church-man to the Mitre,
The shepherd to the Star,
The gardener hies him to the Rose,
To the Drum the man of war ;
To the Feathers, ladies, you ; the Globe
The sea-man doth not scorn :
The usurer to the Devil, and
The townsman to the Horn.
The huntsman to the White Hart,
To the Ship the merchants go,
But you that do the muses love,
The Sign called River Po.
The banquerout to the World's End,
The fool to the Fortune hie,
Unto the Mouth the oyster wife,
The fiddler to the Pie.
The punk unto the Cockatrice,
The drunkard to the Vine,
The beggar to the Bush, then meet,
And with Duke Humphrey dine.

Col. Fair Lucrece, I have brought these lords from court, to feast with thee : sirrah, prepare us dinner.

Luc. My lord is welcome, so are all his friends; The news at court, lords.

Hor. Madam, strange news, Prince Sextus by the enemies of Rome

Was nobly us'd, and made their general.
Twice hath he met his father in the field,
And foil'd him by the warlike Gabines' aid :
But how hath he rewarded that brave nation,
That in his great disgrace supported him ;
I'll tell you, Madam ; he, since the last battle,
Sent to his father a close messenger
To be receiv'd to grace ; withal demanding
What he should do with those his enemies ?
Great Tarquin from his son receives this news,
Being walking in his garden : when the messenger
Importun'd him for answer, the proud king
Lops with his wand the heads of poppies off
And says no more ; with this uncertain answer
The messenger to Sextus back returns,
Who questions of his father's words, looks, gesture ;
He tells him what the haughty speechless king
Did to the heads of poppies, which bold Sextus
Straight apprehends, cuts off the great men's heads,
And having left the Gabines without govern,
Flies to his father, and this day is welcom'd,
For this his traiterous service by the king,
With all due solemn honors, to the court.

Scæ. Courtesy strangely requited ! this none but the son
of Tarquin would have enterpris'd.

Val. I like it, I applaud it ; this will come to somewhat
in the end : when heaven has cast up his account, some of
them will be call'd to a hard reckoning. For my part, I
dreamt last night I went a fishing.

Song.—VALERIUS.

Though the weather jangles
With our hooks and our angles,
 Our nets be shaken and no fish taken ;
Though fresh cod and whiting,
Are not this day biting,
Gurnet, nor conger, to satisfy hunger,
            Yet look to our draught.
Hale the main bowling,
The seas have left their rolling,
The waves their huffing, the winds their puffing ;
Up to the top-mast, boy,
And bring us news of joy ;
Here's no demurring, no fish is stirring,
            Yet something we have caught.

Col. Leave all to heaven.

Enter CLOWN.

Clown. My lords, the best plumporredge in all Rome cools for your honors ; dinner is piping hot upon the table ; and if you make not the more haste, you are like to have but cold cheer : the cook hath done his part ; and there's not a dish on the dresser but he has made it smoke for you : if you have good stomachs, and come not in while the meat is hot, you'll make hunger and cold meet together.

Col. My man's a rhetorician I can tell you,
And his conceit is fluent. Enter, lords ;
You must be Lucrece' guests, and she is scant
In nothing, for such princes must not want.

[exeunt all but Valerius and Clown.

Clown. My Lord Valerius, I have even a suit to your honour; I ha' not the power to part from you, without a relish, a note, a tone; we must get an air betwixt us.

Val. Thy meaning?

Clown. Nothing but this ;—

> John for the king has been in many ballads,
> John for the king down dino ;
> John for the king has eaten many sallads,
> John for the king sings hey ho.

Val. Thou would'st have a song, would'st thou not?

Clown. And be everlastingly bound to your honour; I am now forsaking the world and the devil, and somewhat leaning towards the flesh; if you could but teach me how to choose a wench fit for my stature and complexion, I should rest yours in all good offices.

Val. I'll do that for thee :—what's thy name?

Clown. My name, sir, is Pompey.

Val. Well then, attend.

Song.—VALERIUS.

> Pompey, I will shew thee the way to know
> A dainty dapper wench.
> First see her all bare, let her skin be rare,
> And be touch'd with no part of the French:
> Let her looks be clear, and her brows severe,
> Her eye-brows thin and fine :
> But if she be a punk, and love to be drunk,
> Then keep her still from the wine.
> Let her stature be mean, and her body clean,
> Thou can'st not choose but like her :
> But see she have good clothes, with a fair Roman nose,
> For that's the sign of a striker.

> Let her legs be small, but not us'd to sprawl,
> Her tongue not too loud nor cocket ;*
> Let her arms be strong, and her fingers long,
> But not us'd to dive in a pocket.
> Let her body be long, and her back be strong,
> With a soft lip that entangles ;
> With an ivory breast, and her hair well drest,
> Without gold lace or spangles.
> Let her foot be small, clean legg'd withal,
> Her apparel not too gaudy :
> And one that hath not been in any house of sin,
> Nor place that hath been bawdy.

Clown. But God's me, I am trifling here with you, and dinner cools o' the table, and I am call'd to my attendance. Oh, my sweet Lord Valerius !   [*exeunt.*

SCENE II.

Enter TARQUIN, PORSENNA, TULLIA, SEXTUS, *and* ARUNS.

Tar. Next King Porsenna, whom we tender dearly,
Welcome, young Sextus; thou hast to our yoke
Suppress'd the neck of a proud nation,
The warlike Gabines, enemies to Rome.
    Sex. It was my duty, royal Emperor,
The duty of a subject and a son;
We, at our mother's intercession likewise,
Are now aton'd with Aruns,
Whom we here receive into our bosom.
    Tul. This is done like a kind brother and a natural son.

* Pert.

Aru. We interchange a royal heart with Sextus, and graft us in your love.

Tar. Now, King Porsenna, welcome once more to Tarquin and to Rome.

Por. We are proud of your alliance; Rome is ours,
And we are Rome's; this our religious league
Shall be carv'd firm in characters of brass,
And live for ever to succeeding times.

Tar. It shall, Porsenna; now this league's establish'd,
We will proceed in our determin'd wars,
To bring the neighbour nations under us;
Our purpose is to make young Sextus general
Of all our army; who hath proved his fortunes,
And found them full of favour: we'll begin
With strong Ardea; have you given in charge
To assemble all our captains, and take muster of our
  strong army?

Aru. That business is dispatch'd.

Sex. We have likewise sent for all our best commanders
To take charge according to their merit: Lord Valerius,
Lord Brutus, Cocles, Mutius Scævola,
And Collatine, to make due preparation for such a gallant
  siege.

Tar. This day you shall set forward; Sextus, go,
And let us see your army march along
Before this king and us, that we may view
The puissance of our host, prepar'd already,
To lay high-rear'd Ardea waste and low.

Sex. I shall, my liege.

Tul. Aruns, associate him.

Aru. A rival with my brother in his honors.

                                   [*exeunt Aruns and Sextus.*

Tar. Porsenna shall·behold the strength·of.Rome,
And body of the camp, under the charge
Of two brave·princes, to lay hostile siege
Against the strongest city that withstands
The all-commanding Tarquin.

    Por. 'Tis an object to please Porsenna's eye. [*soft march.*

    Tul. The host is now upon their march.
You from this place may see
The pride of all the Roman chivalry.

SEXTUS, ARUNS, BRUTUS, COLLATINE, VALERIUS, SCÆVOLA, HORATIUS, *with* SOLDIERS; *drums and colours, march over the stage, and congee to the King and Queen.*

    Por. This sight's more pleasing to Porsenna's eye,
Than all our·rich Attalia's* pompous feasts,
Or sumptuous revels : we are born a soldier,
And in our nonage suck'd the milk of war.
Should any strange fate lower upon this army,
Or·that the merciless gulf of confusion
Should swallow them, we at our proper charge,
And from our native confines vow supply
Of men and arms to make these numbers full.

    Tar. You are our royal brother, and in you
Tarquin is powerful and maintains his awe.

    Tul. The like Porsenna may command of Rome.

    Por. But we have, in your fresh varieties,
Feasted too much, and kept ourself too long
From our own seat ; our prosperous return

            * Porsenna was king of Ethuria.

Hath been expected by our lords and peers.

Tar. The business of our wars thus forwarded,
We have best leisure for your entertainment,
Which now shall want no due solemnity.

Por. It hath been beyond both expectation
And merit; but in sight of heaven I swear
If ever royal Tarquin shall demand
Use of our love, 'tis ready stor'd for you,
Even in our kingly breast.

Tar. The like we vow to king Porsenna; we will yet
   a little
Enlarge your royal welcome with varieties,
Such as Rome yields; that done, before we part,
Of two remote dominions make one heart.
Set forward then; our sons wage war abroad,
To make us peace at home; we are of ourself
Without supportance; we all fate defy,
Aidless and of ourself we stand thus high.   *[exeunt.*

SCENE III.

Two SOLDIERS *meet as on the watch.*

1st Sol. Stand, who goes there?

2nd Sol. A friend.

1st Sol. Stir not, for if thou dost, I'll broach thee straight
upon this pike. The word?

2nd Sol. Porsenna.

1st Sol. Pass; stay, who walks the round to night,
The general, or any of his captains?

2nd Sol. Horatius hath the charge: the other chieftains
Rest in the General's tent; there's no commander

Of any note, but revels with the prince;
And I amongst the rest am charg'd t' attend
Upon their rouse.

    1st Sol. Pass freely; I this night must stand
'Twixt them and danger: the time of night?

    2nd Sol. The clock last told eleven.

    1st Sol. The powers celestial,
That have took Rome in charge, protect it still!
Again, good night; thus must poor soldiers do,
Whil'st their commanders are with dainties fed
And sleep on down, the earth must be our bed.   *[exeunt.*

SCENE IV.

A Banquet prepared.

Enter SEXTUS, ARUNS, BRUTUS, VALERIUS, HORATIUS, SCÆVOLA,
and COLLATINE.

    Sex. Sit round: the enemy is pounded fast
In their own folds, the walls, made to oppugn
Hostile incursions, become a prison,
To keep them fast for execution:
There's no eruption to be fear'd.

    Bru. What shall's do? Come, a health to the general's
health; and Valerius, that sits the most civilly, shall begin
it; I cannot talk 'till my blood be mingled with this blood
of grapes. Fill for Valerius; thou should'st drink well, for
thou hast been in the German wars; if thou lov'st me,
drink *upse freeza.**

    Sex. Nay, since Brutus has spoke the word, the first

    * A cant phrase, borrowed from the Dutch, of frequent occurrence in our
dramatic writers, and used to signify being intoxicated. Its derivation is
doubtful, but the most probable interpretation is "in the Dutch fashion."

health shall be imposed on you, Valerius : and if ever you have been Germaniz'd, let it be after the Dutch fashion.

Val. The general may command.

Bru. He may ; why else is he call'd the commander ?

Sex. We will intreat Valerius.

Val. Since you will needs enforce a high German health, look well to your heads, for I come upon you with this Dutch tassaker :* if you were of a more noble science than you are, it will go near to break your heads round.

A Dutch Song. †

O mork giff men ein man,
Skerry merry vip,
O morke giff men ein man
Skerry merry vap,
O morke giff men ein man,
That tik die ten long o drievan ean,
Skerry merry vip, and skerry merry vap,
And skerry merry runke ede bunk,
Ede hoore was a hai dedle downe
Dedle drunke a :
Skerry merry runke ede bunk, ede hoore was drunk a.

O daughter yeis in alto kleene,
Skerry merry vip,
O daughter yeis in alto kleene,
Skerry merry vap,
O daughter yeis in alto kleene,
Ye molten slop. ein yert a leene

---

* *Tassaker*, is perhaps used here to signify a cup or goblet, from the word *tasse*.

† This Anglo-Dutch jargon would not be worth a translation if it were less intelligible than it is.

> Skerry merry vip, and skerry merry vap,
> And skerry merry runk ede bunk,
> Ede hoore was a hey dedle downe
> Dedle drunk a :
> Skerry merry, runke ede bunk ede hoore was drunk a.

Sex. Grammercies ! Valerius, came this high German health as double as his double ruff, I'd pledge it.

Bru. Were it Lubeck, or double double beer, their own natural liquor, I'd pledge it, were it as deep as his ruff: let the health go round about the board, as his band goes round about his neck. I am no more afraid of this Dutch fashion, than I should be of the heathenish invention.

Col. I must entreat you spare me, for my brain brooks not the fumes of wine; their vaporous strength offends me much.

Hor. I would have none spare me, for I'll spare none. Collatine will pledge no health unless it be to his Lucrece.

Sex. What's Lucrece but a woman? and what are women
But tortures and disturbance unto men ?
If they be foul they're odious, and if fair,
They're like rich vessels full of poisonous drugs,
Or like black serpents arm'd with golden scales :
For my own part they shall not trouble me.

Bru. Sextus, sit fast, for I proclaim myself a woman's champion, and shall unhorse thee else.

Val. For my own part I'm a married man, and I'll speak to my wife to thank thee, Brutus.

Aru. I have a wife too, and I think the most virtuous lady in the world.

Sex. I cannot say but that I have a good wife too, and I love her; but if she were in heaven, beshrew me if I would wish her so much hurt as to desire her company upon earth again; yet, upon my honour, though she be not very fair, she is exceeding honest.

Bru. Nay, the less beauty, the less temptation to despoil her honesty.

Sca. I should be angry with him, that should make question of her honour.

Bru. And I angry with thee, if thou should'st not maintain her honour.

Aru. If you compare the virtues of your wives, let me step in for mine.

Col. I should wrong my Lucrece not to stand for her.

Sex. Ha, ha, all captains,
And stand upon the honesty of your wives;
Is't possible, think you, that women of young spirit
And full age, of fluent wit, that can both sing and dance,
Read, write, such as feed well and taste choice cates,
That straight dissolve to purity of blood,
That keep the veins full, and inflame the appetite,
Making the spirit able, strong, and prone,
Can such as these, their husbands being away,
Employ'd in foreign sieges, or elsewhere,
Deny such as importune them at home?
Tell me that flax will not be touch'd with fire,
Nor they be won to what they most desire?

Bru. Shall I end this controversy in a word?

Sex. Do, good Brutus.

Bru. I hold some holy, but some apt to sin;

Some tractable, but some that none can win ;
Such as are virtuous, gold nor wealth can move ;
Some vicious of themselves are prone to love.
Some grapes are sweet, and in the garden grow,
Others, unprun'd, turn wild, neglected so.
The purest ore contains both gold and dross,
The one all gain, the other nought but loss :
The one disgrace, reproach, and scandal taints,
The others angels and sweet featur'd saints.

Col. Such is my virtuous Lucrece.

Aru. Yet she for virtue not comparable to the wife of Aruns ?

Scæ. And why may not mine be rank'd with the most virtuous ?

Hor. I would put in for a lot, but a thousand to one I shall draw but a blank.

Val. I should not shew I lov'd my wife, not to take her part in her absence : I hold her inferior to none.

Aru. Save mine.

Val. No, not to her.

Bru. Oh, this were a brave controversy for a jury of women to arbitrate !

Col. I'll hazard all my fortunes on the virtues
Of divine Lucrece : shall we try them thus?
It is now dead of night ; let's mount our steeds ;
Within this two hours we may reach to Rome,
And to our houses ; all come unprepar'd,
And unexpected by our high prais'd wives ;
She of them all that we find best employ'd,
Devoted, and most housewife-exercis'd,

Let her be held most virtuous, and her husband
Win by the wager a rich horse and armour.

Aru. A hand on that.

Val. Here's a helping hand to that bargain.

Hor. But shall we to horse without circumstance?

Scæ. Scævola will be mounted with the first.

Sex. Then mount cheval. Brutus, this night take you
the charge of the army; I'll see the trial of this wager:
'twould do me good to see some of them find their wives in
the arms of their lovers, they are so confident in their virtues. Brutus, we'll interchange: good night! be thou but
as provident over the army as we, if our horses fail not,
expeditious in our journey: to horse, to horse.

All. Farewell, good Brutus.   [*exeunt.*

SCENE V.

Enter Lucrece *and her two* Maids.

Luc. But one hour more and you shall all to rest:
Now that your lord is absent from this house,
And that the master's eye is from his charge,
We must be careful, and with providence
Guide his domestic business; we have now
Given o'er all feasting, and left revelling,
Which ill becomes the house whose lord is absent.
We banish all excess till his return,
In fear of whom my soul doth daily mourn.

1st. Maid. Madam, so please you, to repose yourself
Within your chamber; leave us to our tasks,
We will not loiter, though you take your rest.

Luc. Not so, you shall not overwatch yourselves
Longer than I wake with you ; for it fits
Good housewives, when their husbands are from home,
To eye their servants' labours, and in care
And the true manage of his household state,
Earliest to rise, and to be up most late.
Since all his business he commits to me,
I'll be his faithful steward till the camp
Dissolve, and he return : thus wives should do ;
In absence of their lords be husbands too.

2nd. Maid. Madam, the lord Turnus his man was thrice for you here, to have entreated you home to supper : he says, his lord takes it unkindly he could not have your company.

Luc. To please a loving husband, I'll offend
The love and patience of my dearest friend :
Methinks his purpose was unreasonable,
To draw me in my husband's absence forth
To feast and banquet : 'twould have ill become me,
To have left the charge of such a spacious house
Without both lord and mistress :
I am opinion'd thus : wives should not stray
Out of their doors, their husbands being away :
Lord Turnus, excuse me.

1st. Maid. Pray, madam, set me right into my work.

Luc. Being abroad, I may forget the charge
Impos'd me by my lord, or be compell'd
To stay out late ; which, were my husband here,
Might be without distaste ; but he from hence,
With late abroad, there can no excuse dispense.

Here, take your work again, a while proceed,
And then to bed, for whilst you sew I'll read.

Enter SEXTUS, ARUNS, VALERIUS, COLLATINE, HORATIUS, *and* SCÆVOLA.

Aru. I would have hazarded all my hopes, my wife had not been so late a revelling.

Val. Nor mine at this time of night a gambling.

Hor. They wear so much cork under their heels they cannot chuse but love to caper.

Scæ. Nothing does me good, but that if my wife were watching, all theirs were wantoning, and if I have lost, none can brag of their winnings.

Sex. Now, Collatine, to yours; either Lucrece must be better employ'd than the rest, or you content to have her virtues rank'd with the rest.

Col. I am pleas'd.

Hor. Soft, soft, let's steal upon her as upon the rest, lest having some watch-word at our arrival, we may give her notice to be better prepar'd : nay, by your leave, Collatine, we'll limit you no advantage.

Col. See, lords, thus Lucrece revels with her maids; instead of riot, quaffing, and the practice of high lavoltoes to the ravishing sound of chamb'ring music, she, like a good housewife, is teaching of her servants sundry chares. * Lucrece?

Luc. My lord and husband, welcome, ten times welcome.
Is it to see your Lucrece you thus late
Have with your person's hazard left the camp,

* *Chare,* work.

And trusted to the danger of a night so dark, and full of
        horror?

Aru. Lords, all's lost.

Hor. By Jovc I'll buy my wife a wheel, and make her
spin for this trick.

Scæ. If I make not mine learn to live by the prick of her
needle for this, I'm no Roman.

Col. Sweet wife, salute these lords; thy continence hath
won thy husband a Barbary horse and a rich coat of
arms.

Luc. O pardon me; the joy to see my lord,
Took from me all respect of their degrees.
The richest entertainment lives with us,
According to the hour and the provision
Of a poor wife in the absence of her husband,
We prostrate to you; howsoever mean,
We thus excuse't; Lord Collatine's away;
We neither feast, dance, quaff, riot, nor play.

Sex. If one woman, among so many bad, may be found
good; if a white wench may prove a black swan, it is
Lucrece; her beauty hath relation to her virtue, and her
virtue correspondent to her beauty, and in both she is
matchless.

Col. Lords, will you yield the wager?

Aru. Stay, the wager was as well which of our wives was
fairest too; it stretch'd as well to their beauty as to their
continence; who shall judge that?

Hor. That can none of us, because we are all parties; let
Prince Sextus determine it who hath been with us, and
been an eye witness of their beauties.

Val. Agreed.

Scæ. I am pleas'd with the censure of Prince Sextus.

Aru. So are we all.

Col. I commit my Lucrece wholly to the dispose of Sextus.

Sex. And Sextus commits him wholly to the dispose of
            Lucrece.

I love the lady and her grace desire,

Nor can my love wrong what my thoughts admire.

Aruns, no question but your wife is chaste,

And thrifty, but this lady knows no waste.

Valerius, yours is modest, something fair,

Her grace and beauty are without compare;

Thine, Mutius, well dispos'd, and of good feature,

But the world yields not so divine a creature;

Horatius, thine a smug lass and grac'd well,

But amongst all, fair Lucrece doth excel.

Then our impartial heart and judging eyes,

This verdict gives, fair Lucrece wins the prize.

Col. Then, lords, you are indebted to me a horse and armour.

All. We yield it.

Luc. Will you taste such welcome, lords, as a poor unprovided house can yield?

Sex. Grammercy, Lucrece, no; we must this night sleep by Ardea's walls.

Luc. But, my lords, I hope my Collatine will not so leave his Lucrece.

Sex. He must; we have but idled from the camp, to try a merry wager about their wives; and this at the hazard of the king's displeasure, should any man be missing from his charge: the powers that govern Rome make divine Lucrece for ever happy. Good night.

Scæ. But, Valerius, what thinkest thou of the country girls from whence we came, compar'd with our city wives whom we this night have try'd?

Val. Scævola, thou shalt hear.

Song.—Valerius.

O yes, room for the cryer,
Who never yet was found a liar.

O ye fine smug country lasses,
That would for brooks change crystal glasses,
And be transhap'd from foot to crown,
And straw beds change for beds of down;
Your partlets* turn into rebatoes,†
And 'stead of carrots eat potatoes;
Your frontlets lay by, and your rails,‡
And fringe with gold your daggl'd tails.
Now your hawk-noses shall have hoods
And billements§ with golden studs:
Straw hats shall be no more bongraces‖
From the bright sun to hide your faces,
For hempen smocks to help the itch,
Have linen sewed with silver stitch;
And wheresoe'er they chance to stride,
One bare before to be their guide.
O yes, room for the cryer,
Who never yet was found a liar.

---

* Ruffs.   † Falling collars.   ‡ Cloaks, or loose gowns.   § Habiliments.
‖ Projecting bonnets to defend the complexion.

Luc. Will not my husband repose this night with me?

Hor. Lucrece shall pardon him, we have took our leaves of our wives; nor shall Collatine be before us though our ladies in other things come behind you.

Col. I must be sway'd: the joys and the delights of many thousand nights meet all in one to make my Lucrece happy.

Luc. I am bound to your strict will; to each, good night!

Sex. To horse, to horse! Lucrece, we cannot rest,
Till our hot lust embosom in thy breast.   [*aside.*

                                [*exeunt all but Lucrece.*

Luc. With no unkindness we should our lords upbraid,
Husbands and kings must always be obey'd.
Nothing save the high business of the state,
And the charge given him at Ardea's siege,
Could have made Collatine so much digress
From the affection that he bears his wife;
But subjects must excuse when kings claim power.
But leaving this, before the charm of sleep
Seize with his downy wings upon my eyes,
I must go take account among my servants
Of their day's task; we must not cherish sloth:
No covetous thought makes me thus provident,
But to shun idleness, which, wise men say,
Begets rank lust, and virtue beats away.   [*exit.*

ACT IV. SCENE I.

Enter Sextus, Aruns, Horatius, Brutus, Scævola,
Collatine, *and* Valerius.

Hor. Return to Rome now we are in the midway to the
camp?

Sex. My lord, 'tis bus'ness that concerns my life.
To-morrow, if we live, we'll visit thee.

Val. Will Sextus enjoin me to accompany him?

Scæ. Or me?

Sex. Nor you, nor any; 'tis important business
And serious occurrences that call me.
Perhaps, lords, I'll commend you to your wives.
Collatine, shall I do you any service to your Lucrece?

Col. Only commend me.

Sex. What! no private token to purchase our kind
welcome?

Col. 'Would royal Sextus would but honour me to bear
her a slight token.

Sex. What?

Col. This ring.

Sex. As I am royal I will see't delivered.
This ring to Lucrece shall my love convey,   [*aside*.
And in this gift thou dost thy bed betray.
To-morrow we shall meet; this night, sweet fate,
May I prove welcome though a guest ingrate!   [*exit*.

Aru. He's for the city, we for the camp; the night
makes the way tedious and melancholy; pr'ythee a merry
song to beguile it.

Song.—VALERIUS.

There was a young man and a maid fell in love,
Terry dery ding, terry dery ding, terry terry dino.
To get her good will he often did
Terry dery ding, terry dery ding, langtido dille ;
There's many will say, and most will allow, terry dery, &c.
There's nothing so good as a terry dery dery, &c.
I would wish all maids before they be sick, terry dery, &c.
To enquire for a young man that has a good terry dery, &c.

Scæ. Nay, my Lord, I heard them all have a conceit of an Englishman; a strange people in the western islands, one that for his variety in habit, humour, and gesture, puts down all other nations whatsoever; a little of that if you love me.

Val. Well, Scævola, you shall.

Song.—VALERIUS.

The Spaniard loves his ancient slop,
The Lombard his Venetian,
And some like breechless women go,
The Russ, Turk, Jew, and Grecian :
The thrifty Frenchman wears small waist,
The Dutch his belly boasteth,
The Englishman is for them all,
And for each fashion coasteth.

The Turk in linen wraps his head,
The Persian his in lawn too,
The Russ with sables furs his cap,
And change will not be drawn to :

The Spaniard's constant to his block,
The French inconstant ever,
But of all felts that can be felt,
Give me your English beaver.

The German loves his coney-wool,
The Irishman his shag too,
The Welch his Monmouth loves to wear,
And of the same will brag too.
Some love the rough, and some the smooth,
Some great, and others small things ;
But, oh, your lecherous Englishman,
He loves to deal in all things.

The Russ drinks quass ; Dutch, Lubeck beer,
And that is strong, and mighty ;
The Briton he metheglin quaffs,
The Irish aqua vitæ ;
The French affects the Orleans' grape,
The Spaniard tastes his sherry,
The English none of these can 'scape,
But he with all makes merry.

The Italian in her high chopine,
Scotch lass, and lovely Frow too,
The Spanish Donna, French Madam,
He will not fear to go to ;
Nothing so full of hazard dread,
Nought lives above the centre,
No fashion, health, no wine, nor wench,
On which he dare not venture.

Hor. Good Valerius, this has brought us even to the
skirts of the camp : enter, lords.   [*exeunt.*

SCENE II.

Enter SEXTUS, LUCRECE, *and* ATTENDANTS.

Luc. This ring, my lord, hath op'd the gates to you;
For though I know you for a royal prince,
My sovereign's son, and friend to Collatine,
Without that key you had not enter'd here.
More lights! and see a banquet straight provided;
My love to my dear husband shall appear
In the kind welcome that I give his friend.

Sex. Not love-sick, but love-lunatic, love-mad:
I am all fire, impatience, and my blood
Boils in my heart, with loose and sensual thoughts. [*aside*.

Luc. A chair for the prince! may't please your highness
sit?

Sex. Madam, with you.

Luc. It will become the wife of Collatine to wait upon
your trencher.

Sex. You shall sit: behind us at the camp we left our
          state;
We're but your guest; indeed, you shall not wait;—
Her modesty hath such strong power o'er me,
And such a reverence hath fate given her brow,
That it appears a kind of blasphemy,
T'have any wanton word harsh in her ears.
I cannot woo, and yet I love 'bove measure;
'Tis force, not suit, must purchase this rich treasure.
                                        [*aside*.

Luc. Your highness cannot taste such homely cates.

Sex. Indeed I cannot feed but on thy face;

Thou art the banquet that my thoughts embrace.   [*aside.*

  Luc. Know you, my lord, what free and zealous welcome
We tender you, your highness would presume
Upon your entertainment: oft, and many times,
I have heard my husband speak of Sextus' valour,
Extol your worth, praise your perfection,
Aye, dote upon your valour, and your friendship prize
Next his Lucrece.

  Sex. Oh impious lust, in all things base, respectless, and
        unjust!
Thy virtue, grace, and fame I must enjoy,
Though in the purchase I all Rome destroy.   [*aside.*
Madam, if I be welcome,
As your virtue bids me presume I am,
Carouse to me a health unto your husband.

  Luc. A woman's draught, my lord, to Collatine.

  Sex. Nay, you must drink off all.

  Luc. Your grace must pardon the tender weakness
Of a woman's brain.

  Sex. It is to Collatine.

  Luc. Methinks 'twould ill become the modesty
Of any Roman lady to carouse,
And drown her virtues in the juice of grapes.
How can I shew my love unto my husband
To do his wife such wrong? by too much wine
I might neglect the charge of this great house,
Left solely to my keep; else my example
Might in my servants breed encouragement
So to offend, both which were pardonless;
Else to your grace I might neglect my duty,

And slack obeisance to so great a guest:
All which being accidental unto wine,
O let me not so wrong my Collatine.

Sex. We excuse you:—her perfections like a torrent
With violence breaks upon me, and at once
Inverts and swallows all that's good in me.
Preposterous fates! what mischiefs you involve
Upon a caitiff prince, left to the fury
Of all grand mischief? hath the grandame world
Yet mother'd* such a strange abortive wonder,
That from her virtues should arise my sin?
I am worse than what's most ill, depriv'd all reason,
My heart all fiery lust, my soul all treason.   [*aside.*

Luc. My lord, I fear your health, your changing brow
Hath shewn so much disturbance: noble Sextus,
Hath not your vent'rous travel from the camp,
Nor the moist rawness of this humorous night,
Impair'd your health?

Sex. Divinest Lucrece, no: 1 cannot eat.

Luc. To rest then;
A rank of torches there attend the prince!

Sex. Madam, I doubt I am a guest, this night,
Too troublesome, and I offend your rest.

Luc. This ring speaks for me, that, next Collatine,
You are to me most welcome; yet, my lord,
Thus much presume, without this from his hand,
Sextus this night could not have enter'd here:
No, not the king himself;
My doors the day time to my friends are free,

* * *

* *Smother'd;* in the former editions.

But in the night the obdure gates are less kind;
Without this ring they can no entrance find.
Lights for the prince!

Sex. A kiss, and so good night; nay, for your ring's
sake, deny not that.

Luc. Jove give your highness soft and sweet repose!

Sex. And thee the like, with soft and sweet content!
My vows are fix'd, my thoughts on mischief bent. [*aside.*

           [*exit with torches.*

Luc. 'Tis late; so many stars shine in this room,
By reason of this great and princely guest,
The world might call our modesty in question,
To revel thus, our husband at the camp;
Haste, and to rest; save in the prince's chamber,
Let not a light appear: my heart's all sadness.
Jove! unto thy protection I commit
My chastity and honour, to thy keep
My waking soul I give, whilst my thoughts sleep.

         [*exit, with attendants.*

SCENE III.

Enter CLOWN *and a* SERVING MAN.

Clown. Soft, soft, not too loud; imagine we were now
going on the ropes with eggs on our heels; he that hath
but a creaking shoe I would he had a creak in his neck:
tread not too hard for disturbing Prince Sextus.

Ser. I wonder the prince would have none of us stay in
his chamber and help him to bed.

Clown. What an ass art thou to wonder! there may be
many causes: thou know'st the prince is a soldier, and sol-

diers many time want shift: who can say whether he have a clean shirt on or no? for any thing that we know he hath us'd staves-acre,* or hath ta'en a medicine to kill the itch; what's that to us? we did our duty to proffer ourselves.

Ser. And what should we enter farther into his thoughts? come, shall's to bed? I'm as drowsy as a dormouse, and my head is as heavy as though I had a night-cap of lead on.

Clown. And my eyes begin to glue themselves together; I was, till supper was done, altogether for your repast, and now, after supper, I am only for your repose: I think, for the two virtues of eating and sleeping, there's never a Roman spirit under the cope of heaven can put me down.

Enter MIRABLE.

Mir. For shame! what a conjuring and catter-wawling keep you here, that my lady cannot sleep: you shall have her call by and by, and send you all to bed with a witness.

Clown. Sweet Mistress Mirable, we are going.

Mir. You are too loud; come, every man dispose him to his rest, and I'll to mine.

Ser. Out with your torches.

Clown. Come then, and every man sneak into his kennel.

[*exeunt.*

SCENE IV.

Enter SEXTUS, *with his sword drawn, and a taper lighted.*

Sex. Night, be as secret as thou art close, as close
As thou art black and dark! thou ominous queen
Of tenebrous silence, make this fatal hour
As true to rape, as thou hast made it kind

* The herb larkspur.

To murder, and harsh mischief! Cynthia, mask thy cheek,
And all you sparkling elemental fires,
Choak up your beauties in prodigious fogs,
Or be extinct in some thick vaporous clouds,
Lest ye behold my practice! I am bound
Upon a black adventure, on a deed
That must wound virtue, and make beauty bleed.
Pause, Sextus, and before thou run'st thyself
Into this violent danger, weigh thy sin:
Thou art yet free, belov'd, grac'd in the camp;
Of great opinion and undoubted hope;
Rome's darling in the universal grace,
Both of the field, and senate, where these fortunes
Do make thee great in both:* back! yet thy fame
Is free from hazard, and thy style from shame.
O fate! thou hast usurp'd such power o'er man,
That where thou plead'st thy will, no mortal can.
On then black mischief, hurry me the way!
Myself I must destroy, her life betray.
The hate† of king and subject, the displeasure
Of prince and people, the revenge of noble,
And contempt of base; the incurr'd vengeance
Of my wrong'd kinsman Collatine, the treason
Against divin'st Lucrece; all these total curses
Foreseen, not fear'd, upon one Sextus meet,
To make my days harsh, so this night be sweet.

* In the quartos, this and the preceding line stand thus:

      " Both of the field and senate; were these fortunes
        To make thee great in both," &c.

† *Ib.*—State.

No jar of clock, no ominous hateful howl
Of any starting hound, no horse-cough breath'd from the
      entrails
Of any drowsy groom, wakes this charm'd silence,
And starts this general slumber; forward still.

                        [*Lucrece discovered in her bed.*

To make thy lust live, all thy virtues kill.
Here, here, behold! beneath these curtains lies
That bright enchantress that hath daz'd my eyes.
Oh, who but Sextus could commit such waste
On one so fair, so kind, so truly chaste?
Or like a ravisher thus rudely stand,
To offend this face, this brow, this lip, this hand?
Or at such fatal hours these revels keep,
With thought once to defile thy innocent sleep?
Save in this breast such thoughts could find no place,
Or pay, with treason, her hospitable grace;
But I am lust-burnt all, bent on what's bad;
That, which should calm good thought, makes Tarquin
      mad.
Madam! Lucrece!

  Luc. Whose that? oh me! beshrew you.

  Sex. Sweet, 'tis I.

  Luc. What I?

  Sex. Make room.

  Luc. My husband Collatine?

  Sex. Thy husband's at the camp.

  Luc. Here is no place for any man save him.

  Sex. Grant me that grace.

  Luc. What are you?

Sex. Tarquin and thy friend, and must enjoy thee.

Luc. Heaven such sins defend!

Sex. Why do you tremble, lady? cease this fear;
I am alone; there's no suspicious ear
That can betray this deed: nay, start not, sweet.

Luc. Dream I, or am I full awake? oh no!
I know I dream to see Prince Sextus so.
Sweet lord, awake me, rid me from this terror:
I know you for a prince, a gentleman,
Royal and honest, one that loves my lord,
And would not wrack a woman's chastity
For Rome's imperial diadem: oh then
Pardon this dream! for being awake, I know
Prince Sextus, Rome's great hope, would not for shame
Havock his own worth, or despoil my fame.

Sex. I'm bent on both; my thoughts are all on fire;
Choose thee, thou must embrace death, or desire.
Yet do I love thee; wilt thou accept it?

Luc. No.

Sex. If not thy love, thou must enjoy thy foe.
Where fair means cannot, force shall make my way:
By Jove, I must enjoy thee.

Luc. Sweet lord, stay.

Sex. I'm all impatience, violence, and rage,
And save thy bed, nought can this fire assuage:
Wilt love me?

Luc. No, I cannot.

Sex. Tell me why?

Luc. Hate me, and in that hate first let me die.

Sex. By Jove, I'll force thee.

Luc. By a god you swear
To do a devil's deed; sweet lord, forbear.
By the same Jove I swear, that made this soul,
Never to yield unto an act so foul.
Help! help!
Sex. These pillows first shall stop thy breath,
If thou but shriekest; hark! how I'll frame thy death.
Luc. For death I care not, so I keep unstain'd
The uncraz'd honour I have yet maintain'd.
Sex. Thou canst keep neither, for if thou but squeak'st,
Or let'st the least harsh noise jar in my ear,
I'll broach thee on my steel; that done, straight murder
One of thy basest grooms, and lay you both
Grasp'd arm in arm on thy adulterate bed,
Then call in witness of that mechall* sin :
So shalt thou die, thy death be scandalous,
Thy name be odious, thy suspected body
Deny'd all funeral rites, and loving Collatine
Shall hate thee even in death : then save all this,
And to thy fortunes add another friend,
Give thy fears comfort, and these torments end.
Luc. I'll die first; and yet hear me, as you're noble
If all your goodness and best generous thoughts
Be not exil'd your heart, pity, oh pity
The virtues of a woman ! mar not that
Cannot be made again : this once defil'd,
Not all the ocean waves can purify
Or wash my stain away; you seek to soil

---

* Probably derived from the French word *mechant*, wicked.

That which the radiant splendor of the sun
Cannot make bright again; behold my tears,
Oh think them pearl'd drops, distilled from the heart
Of soul-chaste Lucrece; think them orators,
To plead the cause of absent Collatine, your friend and
       kinsman.

  Sex. Tush, I am obdure.

  Luc. Then make my name foul, keep my body pure.
Oh, prince of princes, do but weigh your sin:
Think how much I shall lose, how small you win.
I lose the honour of my name and blood,
Loss Rome's imperial crown cannot make good.
You win the world's shame and all good men's hate;
Oh! would you pleasure buy at such dear rate?
Nor can you term it pleasure, for what is sweet,
Where force and hate, jar and contention meet?
Weigh but for what 'tis that you urge me still,
To gain a woman's love against her will?
You'll but repent such wrong done a chaste wife,
And think that labour's not worth all your strife;
Curse your hot lust, and say you've wrong'd your friends,
But all the world cannot make me amends:
I took you for a friend, wrong not my trust,
But let these chaste tears quench your fiery lust.

  Sex. No, those moist tears contending with my fire,
Quench not my heat but make it climb much higher;
I'll drag thee hence.

  Luc. Oh!

  Sex. If thou raise these cries, lodg'd in thy slaughter'd
Arms some base groom dies.

And Rome that hath admir'd thy name so long
Shall blot thy death with scandal from my tongue.

Luc. Jove guard my innocence!

Sex. Lucrece, thou art mine,
In spite of Jove and all the powers divine.

[*he bears her out.*

SCENE V.

Enter a SERVING MAN.

Ser. What's o'clock, trow? my lord bad me be early ready with my gelding, for he would ride betimes in the morning: now had I rather be up an hour before my time than a minute after, for my lord will be so infinite angry if I but oversleep myself a moment, that I had better be out of my life than in his displeasure; but soft, some of my lord Collatine's men lie in the next chamber, I care not if I call them up, for it grows towards day: what! Pompey, Pompey?

Clown. [*within.*] Who is that calls?

Enter CLOWN.

Ser. 'Tis I.

Clown. Who's that? my lord Sextus his man? what a pox make you up before day?

Ser. I would have the key of the gate to come at my lord's horse in the stable.

Clown. I would my lord Sextus and you were both in the hay-loft, for Pompey can take none of his natural rest among you; here's e'en ostler rise and give my horse another peck of hay.

Ser. Nay, good Pompey, help me to the key of the stable.

Bru. Methinks, our wars go not well forwards, Horatius ; we have greater enemies to bustle with than the Ardeans, if we durst but front them.

Hor. Would it were come to fronting !

Bru. Then we married men should have the advantage of the bachelors, Horatius, especially such as have reveling wives, those that can caper in the city, while their husbands are in the camp. Collatine, why are you so sad? the thought of this should not trouble you, having a Lucrece to your bedfellow.

Col. My lord, I know no cause of discontent, yet cannot I be merry.

Scæ. Come, come, make him merry, let's have a song in praise of his Lucrece.

Val. Content.

Song—VALERIUS.

On two white columns arch'd she stands,
   Some snow would think them sure ;
Some chrystal, others lillies stript,
   But none of those so pure.

This beauty when I contemplate,
   What riches I behold,
'Tis roof'd within with virtuous thoughts,
   Without 'tis thatch'd with gold.

Two doors there are to enter at,
   The one I'll not enquire,
Because conceal'd, the other seen,
   Whose sight inflames desire.

Whether the porch be coral clear,
  Or with rich crimson lin'd,
Or rose-leaves, lasting all the year,
  It is not yet divin'd.

Her eyes not made of purest glass,
  Or chrystal, but transpareth ;
The life of diamonds they surpass,
  Their very sight ensnareth.

That which without we rough-cast call,
  To stand 'gainst wind and weather,
For it's rare beauty equals all
  That I have nam'd together.

For were it not by modest art
  Kept from the sight of skies,
It would strike dim the sun itself,
  And daze the gazers' eyes.

The case so rich, how may we praise
  The jewel lodg'd within,
To draw their praise I were unwise,
  To wrong them, it were sin.

Aru. I should be frolick if my brother were but return'd to the camp.

Hor. And in good time; behold prince Sextus.

Enter SEXTUS.

All. Health to our general !

Sex. Thank you.

Bru. Will you survey your forces, and give order for a present assault ? your soldiers long to be tugging with the Ardeans.

Sex. No.

Col. Have you seen Lucretia, my lord, how fares she ?

Sex. Well; I'll to my tent.

Aru. Why, how now; what's the matter, brother ?

                              [exeunt Sextus and Aruns.

Bru. Thank you ; no.   Well, I'll to my tent : get thee to thy tent, and coward go with thee, if thou hast no more spirit to a speedy encounter.

Val. Shall I go after him, and know the cause of his discontent ?

Sca. Or I, my lord ?

Bru. Neither; to pursue a fool in his humour is the next way to make him more humorous; I'll not be guilty of his folly, thank you, no; before I wish him health again, when he is sick of the sullens, may I die, not like a Roman, but like a runagate.

Sca. Perhaps he's not well.

Bru. Well: then let him be ill.

Val. Nay if he be dying as I could wish he were, I'll ring out his funeral peal, and this it is.

Song.—VALERIUS.

Come, list and hark,
  The bell doth toll
For some but new
  Departing soul.
And was not that
  Some ominous fowl,
The bat, the night-
  Crow or screech-owl ?

To these I hear
　　The wild wolf howl,
In this black night
　　That seems to scowl.
All these my black -
　　Book shall enroll,
For, hark, still, still,
　　The bell doth toll
For some but now
　　Departing soul.

Scæ. Excellent, Valerius; but is not that Collatine's man?

Enter CLOWN.

Val. The news with this hasty post.

Clown. Did nobody see my lord Collatine? oh! my lady commends her to you; here's a letter.

Col. Give it me.

Clown. Fie upon't, never was poor Pompey so over-labour'd as I have been; I think I have spurr'd my horse such a question, that he is scarce able to wig or wag his tail for an answer: but my lady bad. me spare for no horseflesh, and I think I have made him run his race.

Bru. Cousin Collatine, the news at Rome?

Col. Nothing but what you all may well partake; read here, my lord.

Brutus reads the letter.

Dear lord, if ever thou wilt see thy Lucrece,
Choose of the friends which thou affectest best,
And, all important business set apart,
Repair to Rome : commend me to lord Brutus,

Valerius, Mutius, and Horatius.
Say I entreat their presence, where my father
Lucretius shall attend them ; farewell, sweet,
Th' affairs are great, then do not fail to meet.

   Bru. I'll thither as I live.   [*exit.*

   Col. I, though I die.   [*exit.*

   Scæ. To Rome with expeditious wings we'll fly.   [*exit.*

   Hor. The news, the news, if it have any shape
Of sadness, if some prodigy have chanc'd,
That may beget revenge, I'll cease to chafe,
Vex, martyr, grieve, torture, torment myself,
And tune my humour to strange strains of mirth,
My soul divines some happiness ; speak, speak :
I know thou hast some news that will create me
Merry and musical, for I would laugh,
Be new trans-shap'd ; I pr'ythee sing, Valerius,
That I may air with thee.

*Song—*Valerius.

I'd think myself as proud in shackles,
As doth the ship in all her tackles.
The wise man boasts no more his brains,
Than I'd exult in gyves and chains :
As creditors would use their debtors,
So could I toss and shake my fetters,
But not confess ; my thoughts should be
In durance fast as those kept me.
And could, when spite their hearts environs,
Then dance to th' music of my irons.

   Val. Now tell us what's the project of thy message?

   Clown. My lords, the princely Sextus has been at home,

but what he hath done there I may partly mistrust, but cannot altogether resolve you : besides, my lady swore me, that whatsoever I suspected I should say nothing.

Val. If thou wilt not say thy mind, I pr'ythee sing thy mind, and then thou may'st save thine oath.

Clown. Indeed I was not sworn to that; I may either laugh out my news, or sing 'em, and so I may save mine oath to my lady.

Hor. How's all at Rome, that with such sad presage
Disturbed Collatine and noble Brutus
Are hurry'd from the camp with Scævola?
And we with expedition 'mongst the rest
Are charg'd to Rome? speak, what did Sextus there
With thy fair mistress?

Val. Second me, my lord, and we'll urge him to disclose it.

VALERIUS, HORATIUS, *and the* CLOWN,—*their Catch.*

> *Val.* Did he take fair Lucrece by the toe, man?
> *Hor.* Toe, man?
> *Val.* Aye, man.
> *Clown.* Ha ha ha ha ha, man.
> *Hor.* And further did he strive to go, man?
> *Clown.* Go, man?
> *Hor.* Aye, man.
> *Clown.* Ha ha ha ha, man, fa derry derry down, ha fa
>   derry dino.
> *Val.* Did he take fair Lucrece by the heel, man?
> *Clown.* Heel, man?
> *Val.* Aye, man.
> *Clown.* Ha ha ha ha, man.
> *Hor.* And did he further strive to feel, man?

Clown. Feel, man ?

Hor. Aye, man.

Clown. Ha ha ha ha, man, ha fa derry, &c.

Val. Did he take the lady by the shin, man ?

Clown. Shin, man ?

Val. Aye, man.

Clown. Ha ha ha ha, man.

Hor. Further too would he have been, man ?

Clown. Been, man ?

Hor. Aye, man.

Clown. Ha ha ha ha, man, ha fa dery, &c.

Val. Did he take the lady by the knee, man ?

Clown. Knee, man ?

Val. Aye, man.

Clown. Ha ha ha ha, man.

Hor. Farther than that would he be, man ?

Clown. Be, man ?

Hor. Aye, man.

Clown. Ha ha ha ha, man, hey fa dery, &c.

Val. Did he take the lady by the thigh, man ?

Clown. Thigh, man ?

Val. Aye, man.

Clown. Ha ha ha ha, man.

Hor. And now he came it somewhat nigh, man ?

Clown. Nigh, man ?

Hor. Aye, man.

Clown. Ha ha ha ha, man, hey fa derry, &c.

Val. But did he do the t'other thing, man ?

Clown. Thing, man ?

Val. Aye, man.

Clown. Ha ha ha ha, man.

Hor. And at the same had he a fling, man ?

Clown. Fling, man ?
Hor. Aye man.
Clown. Ha ha ha, man, hey fa derry, &c.   [*exeunt.*

ACT V.   SCENE I.

A table and a chair covered with black.

LUCRECE *and her* MAID.

Luc. Mirable.
Maid. Madam.
Luc. Is not my father, old Lucretius, come yet?
Maid. Not yet.
Luc. Nor any from the camp?
Maid. Neither, madam.
Luc. Go, begone, and leave me to the truest grief of heart,
That ever enter'd any matron's breast: Oh!
Maid. Why weep you, lady? alas! why do you stain
Your modest cheeks with these offensive tears?
Luc. Nothing, nay, nothing: oh, you powerful gods,
That should have angels guardants on your throne,
To protect innocence and chastity! oh, why
Suffer you such inhuman massacre
Of harmless virtue? wherefore take you charge
Of sinless souls to see them wounded thus
With rape and violence? or give white innocence
Armour of proof 'gainst sin, or by oppression
Kill virtue quite, and guerdon base transgression.
Is it my fate above all other women?
Or is my sin more heinous than the rest,
That amongst thousands, millions, infinites,

I, only I, should to this shame be born,
To be a stain to women, nature's scorn? oh!
 Maid. What ails you, madam? truth, you make me weep
To see you shed salt tears: what hath oppress'd you?
Why is your chamber hung with mourning black?
Your habit sable, and your eyes thus swoln
With ominous tears; alas! what troubles you?
 Luc. I am not sad; thou didst deceive thyself;
I did not weep, there's nothing troubles me:
But wherefore dost thou blush?
 Maid. Madam, not I.
 Luc. Indeed thou didst,
And in that blush my guilt thou did'st betray;
How cam'st thou by the notice of my sin?
 Maid. What sin?
 Luc. My blot, my scandal, and my shame:
O Tarquin! thou my honour did'st betray;
Disgrace, no time, no age, can wipe away; oh!
 Maid. Sweet lady, cheer yourself; I'll fetch my viol,
And see if I can sing you fast asleep:
A little rest would wear away this passion.
 Luc. Do what thou wilt, I can command no more;
Being no more a woman, I am now
Devote to death and an inhabitant
Of th' other world: these eyes must ever weep
Till fate hath clos'd them with eternal sleep.

Enter BRUTUS, COLLATINE, HORATIUS, SCÆVOLA, VALERIUS,
  one way, and OLD LUCRETIUS *another way.*

 O. Luc. Brutus!
 Bru. Lucretius!

Luc. Father!

Col. Lucrece!

Luc. Collatine!

Bru. How cheer you, madam? how is't with you, cousin?
Why is your eye deject and drown'd in sorrow?
Why is this funeral black, and ornaments
Of widow-hood? resolve me, cousin Lucrece.

Hor. How fare you, lady?

O. Luc. What's the matter, girl?

Col. Why, how is't with you, Lucrece? tell me, sweet,
Why dost thou hide thy face, and with thy hand
Darken those eyes that were my suns of joy,
To make my pleasures flourish in the spring?

Luc. Oh me!

Val. Whence are these sighs and tears?

Scæ. How grows this passion?

Bru. Speak, lady, you are hemm'd in with your friends,
Girt in a pale of safety, and environ'd
And circl'd in a fortress of your kindred.
Let not those drops fall fruitless to the ground,
Nor let your sighs add to the senseless wind;
Speak! who hath wrong'd you?

Luc. Ere I speak my woe,
Swear you'll revenge poor Lucrece on her foe.

Bru. Be his head arch'd with gold!

Hor. Be his hand arm'd with an imperial sceptre!

O. Luc. Be he great as Tarquin, thron'd in an imperial
seat!

Bru. Be he no more than mortal, he shall feel
The vengeful edge of this victorious steel.

Luc. Then seat you, lords, whilst I express my wrong !
Father, dear husband, and my kinsmen lords,
Hear me; I am dishonour'd and disgrac'd ;
My reputation mangled, my renown
Disparag'd; but my body, oh my body !
   Col. What, Lucrece ?
   Luc. Stain'd, polluted, and defil'd.
Strange steps are found in my adulterate bed ;
And though my thoughts be white as innocence,
Yet is my body soil'd with lust-burn'd sin,
And by a stranger I am strumpeted,
Ravish'd, enforc'd, and am no more to rank
Among the Roman matrons.
   Bru. Yet cheer you, lady, and restrain these tears ;
If you were forc'd, the sin concerns not you ;
A woman's born but with a woman's strength :
Who was the ravisher ?
   Hor. Aye, name him, lady !
Our love to you shall only thus appear
In the revenge that we will take on him.
   Luc. I hope so, lords ; 'twas Sextus, the king's son.
   All. How ? Sextus Tarquin !
   Luc. That unprincely prince,
Who, guest-wise, enter'd with my husband's ring.
This ring, O Collatine ! this ring you sent,
Is cause of all my woe, your discontent.
I feasted him, then lodg'd him, and bestow'd
My choicest welcome ; but in the dead of night
My traitorous guest came arm'd unto my bed,
Frighted my silent sleep, threaten'd, and pray'd

For entertainment : I despised both ;
Which, hearing, his sharp pointed scimitar,
The tyrant bent against my naked breast.
Alas ! I begg'd my death ; but note his tyranny ;
He brought with him a torment worse than death,
For having murder'd me, he swore to kill
One of my basest grooms, and lodge him dead
In my dead arms : then call in testimony
Of my adultery, to make me hated
Even in my death, of husband, father, friends,
Of Rome, and all the world : :
This, this, O princes ! ravish'd and kill'd me at once.
  Col. Yet comfort, lady,
I quit thy guilt, for what could Lucrece do
More than a woman ? had'st thou dy'd polluted
By this base scandal, thou had'st wrong'd thy fame :
And hinder'd us of a most just revenge.
  All. What shall we do, lords ?
  Bru. Lay your resolute hands
Upon the sword of Brutus : vow and swear,
As you hope meed for merit from the gods,
Or fear reward for sin from devils below ;
As you are Romans, and esteem your fame
More than your lives, all humorous toys set off,
Of madding, singing, smiling, and what else,
Revive your native valours, be yourselves,
And join with Brutus in the just revenge
Of this chaste ravish'd lady ; swear !
  All. We do.
  Luc. Then with your humours, here my grief ends too ;

My stain I thus wipe off, call in my sighs,
And in the hope of this revenge, forbear
Even to my death to fall one passionate tear;
Yet, lords, that you may crown my innocence
With your best thoughts, that you may henceforth know
We are the same in heart, we seem in show:
And though I quit my soul of all such sin,

        [the lords whisper.

I'll not debar my body punishment:
Let all the world learn of a Roman dame,
To prize her life less than her honor'd fame. *[stabs herself.*

 O. Luc. Lucrece!
 Col. Wife!
 Bru. Lady!
 Scæ. She hath slain herself!
 Val. Oh see yet, lords, if there be hope of life.
 Bru. She's dead! then turn your funeral tears to fire
And indignation; let us now redeem
Our mis-spent time, and overtake our sloth
With hostile expedition; this, great lords,
This bloody knife, on which her chaste blood flow'd,
Shall not from Brutus, till some strange revenge
Fall on the heads of Tarquins.
 Hor. Now's the time to call their pride to count:
Brutus, lead on, we'll follow thee to their confusion.
 Val. By Jove, we will; the sprightful youth of Rome,
Trick'd up in plumed harness, shall attend
The march of Brutus, whom we here create
Our general against the Tarquins.
 Scæ. Be it so.

Bru. We embrace it; now to stir the wrath of Rome,
You, Collatine, and good Lucretius,
With eyes yet drown'd in tears, bear that chaste body
Into the market place: that horrid object
Shall kindle them with a most just revenge.

Hor. To see the father and the husband mourn
O'er this chaste dame, that have so well deserv'd
Of Rome and them; then to infer the pride,
The wrongs, and the perpetual tyranny
Of all the Tarquins, Servius Tullius' death,
And his unnatural usage by that monster
Tullia, the queen: all these shall well concur
In a combin'd revenge.

Bru. Lucrece, thy death we'll mourn in glittering arms
And plumed casques: bear that reverend load
Unto the Forum, where our force shall meet
To set upon the palace, and expel
This vip'rous brood from Rome: I know the people
Will gladly embrace our fortunes: Scævola,
Go you and muster powers in Brutus' name.
Valerius, you assist him instantly,
And to the 'mazed people freely speak
The cause of this concourse.

Val. We go.   *[exeunt Valerius and Scævola.*

Bru. And you, dear lords, [*to Collatine and Lucretius.*]
    whose speechless grief is boundless,
Turn all your tears, with ours, to wrath and rage;
The hearts of all the Tarquins shall weep blood
Upon the funeral hearse, with whose chaste body
Honour your arms, and to th' assembled people

Disclose her innocent wounds: Gramercies, lords,

    [*a great shout, and a flourish with drums and trumpets.*

That universal shout tells me their words

Are gracious with the people, and their troops

Are ready embattl'd and expect but us

To lead them on; Jove give our fortunes speed!

We'll murder murder, and base rape shall bleed. [*exeunt.*

SCENE II.

Alarum—Enter in the fight TARQUIN *and* TULLIA *flying, pursued
by* BRUTUS; *the* ROMANS *march with drum and colours;* POR-
SENNA, ARUNS, SEXTUS, TARQUIN, *and* TULLIA, *meet and join
with them; to them,* BRUTUS *and the* ROMANS, *with drum and
soldiers: they make a stand.*

  Bru. Even thus far, tyrant, have we dogg'd thy steps,
Frighting thy queen and thee with horrid steel.

  Tar. Lodg'd in the safety of Porsenna's arms,
Now, traitor Brutus, we dare front thy pride.

  Hor. Porsenna, thou'rt unworthy of a sceptre,
To shelter pride, lust, rape, and tyranny,
In that proud prince and his confederate peers.

  Sex. Traitors to heaven, to Tarquin, Rome, and us!
Treason to kings doth stretch even to the gods;
And those high gods that take great Rome in charge,
Shall punish your rebellion.

  Col. O devil, Sextus! speak not thou of gods,
Nor cast those false and feigned eyes to heaven,
Whose rape the furies must torment in hell,
Of Lucrece, Lucrece!

  Scæ. Her chaste blood still cries

For vengeance to the etherial deities.

   O. Luc. Oh, 'twas a foul deed, Sextus !

   Val. And thy shame
Shall be eternal and outlive her fame.

   Aru. Say Sextus lov'd her, was she not a woman ?
Aye, and perhaps was willing to be forc'd.
Must you, being private subjects, dare to ring
War's loud alarum 'gainst your potent king ?

   Por. Brutus, therein thou dost forget thyself,
And wrong'st the glory of thine ancestors,
Staining thy blood with treason.

   Bru. Tuscan, know
The consul, Brutus, is their powerful foe.

   All the Tarquins. Consul !

   Hor. Aye, consul ; and the powerful hand of Rome
Grasps his imperial sword : the name of king
The tyrant Tarquins have made odious
Unto this nation, and the general knee
Of this our warlike people, now low bends
To royal Brutus where the king's name ends.

   Bru. Now, Sextus, where's the oracle ? when I kiss'd
My mother Earth, it plainly did foretell
My noble virtues did thy sin exceed,
Brutus should sway, and lust-burn'd Tarquin bleed.

   Val. Now shall the blood of Servius fall as heavy
As a huge mountain on your tyrant heads,
O'erwhelming all your glory.

   Hor. Tullia's guilt shall be by us reveng'd, that, in her
       pride,
In blood paternal her rough coach-wheels dy'd.

Luc. Your tyrannies,—

Scæ. Pride,

Col. And my Lucrece' fate,

Shall all be swallow'd in this hostile hate.

Sex. Oh! Romulus, thou, that first rear'd yon walls,

In sight of which we stand, in thy soft bosom

Is hugg'd the nest in which the Tarquins build;

Within the branches of thy lofty spires

Tarquin shall perch, or where he once hath stood,

His high built aëry shall be drown'd in blood;

Alarum then, Brutus! by heaven I vow,

My sword shall prove thou ne'er wast mad till now.

Bru. Sextus, my madness with your lives expires;

Thy sensual eyes are fix'd upon that wall

Thou ne'er shalt enter, Rome confines you all.

Por. A charge then!

Tar. Jove and Tarquin!

Hor. But we cry a Brutus!

Bru. Lucrece, fame, and victory!   [*exeunt.*

SCENE III.

Alarum, the Romans are beaten off.

Enter BRUTUS, HORATIUS, VALERIUS, SCÆVOLA, LUCRETIUS, *and*
COLLATINE.

Bru. Thou Jovial hand, hold up thy sceptre high,

And let not justice be oppress'd with pride;

O you, Penates, leave not Rome and us,

Grasp'd in the purple hands of death and ruin;

The Tarquins have the best.

Hor. Yet stand, my foot is fix'd upon this bridge;

Tiber, thy arched streams shall be chang'd crimson
With Roman blood, before I budge from hence.

Scæ. Brutus, retire; for if thou enter Rome
We are all lost, stand not on valour now,
But save thy people; let's survive this day,
To try the fortunes of another field.

Val. Break down the bridge, lest the pursuing enemy
Enter with us and take the spoil of Rome.

Hor. Then break behind me, for by heaven I'll grow
And root my foot as deep as to the centre,
Before I leave this passage.

Luc. Come, you're mad.

Col. The foe comes on, and we, in trifling here,
Hazard ourselves and people.

Hor. Save them all;
To make Rome stand, Horatius here will fall.

Bru. We would not lose thee; do not breast thyself
'Gainst thousands; if thou front'st them, thou art ring'd
With million swords and darts, and we behind
Must break the bridge of Tiber to save Rome.
Before thee infinite gaze on thy face,
And menace death; the raging streams of Tiber
Are at thy back to swallow thee.

Hor. Retire!
To make Rome live 'tis death that I desire.

Bru. Then farewell, dead Horatius! think in us
The universal arm of potent Rome
Takes his last leave of thee in this embrace.

[all embrace him.

Hor. Farewell!

All. Farewell !

Bru. These arches all must down
To interdict their passage through the town.   [*exeunt.*

SCENE IV.

Alarum.   Enter TARQUIN, PORSENNA, *and* ARUNS, *with their
pikes and Targeters.*

All. Enter, enter, enter !
                    [*a noise of knocking down the bridge within.*

Hor. Soft, Tarquin, see a bulwark to the bridge
You first must pass ; the man that enters here
Must make his passage through Horatius' breast ;
See, with this target do I buckler Rome,
And with this sword defy the puissant army
Of two great kings.

Por. One man to face a host !
Charge, soldiers ! Of full forty thousand Romans
There's but one daring hand against your host,
To keep you from the sack or spoil of Rome ;
Charge, charge !

Aru. Upon them, soldiers !   [*alarum.*

Enter in several places, SEXTUS *and* VALERIUS *above.*

Sex. Oh ! cowards, slaves, and vassals ! what ! not enter?
Was it for this you plac'd my regiment
Upon a hill, to be the sad spectator
Of such a general cowardice ? Tarquin, Aruns,
Porsenna, soldiers, pass Horatius quickly,
For they behind him will devolve the bridge,
And raging Tiber, that's impassable,
Your host must swim before you conquer Rome.

Val. Yet stand, Horatius; bear but one brunt more,
The arched bridge shall sink upon his piles,
And in his fall lift thy renown to heaven.
   Sex. Yet enter.
   Val. Dear Horatius, yet stand
And save a million by one powerful hand.
                        [alarum, and the falling of a bridge.
   Aruns and all. Charge, charge, charge !
   Sex. Degenerate slaves ! the bridge is fall'n, Rome's lost.
   Val. Horatius, thou art stronger than their host;
Thy strength is valour, their's are idle braves;
Now save thyself, and leap into the waves.
   Hor. Porsenna, Tarquin, now wade past your depths
And enter Rome; I feel my body sink
Beneath my pond'rous weight; Rome is preserv'd,
And now farewell : for he that follows me
Must search the bottom of this raging stream.
Fame, with thy golden wings renown my crest,
And Tiber take me on thy silver breast.
                        [he leaps into the river.
   Por. He's leap'd off from the bridge, and drown'd himself.
   Sex. You are deceiv'd, his spirit soars too high
To be choak'd in with the base element
Of water; lo ! he swims, arm'd as he is,
Whilst all the army have discharg'd their arrows,
Of which the shield upon his back sticks full.   *[flourish.*
And hark ! the shout of all the multitude
Now welcomes him a-land : Horatius' fame
Hath check'd our armies with a general shame;
But come, to morrow's fortune must restore

This scandal; which I of the gods implore.

Por. Then we must find another time, fair prince,
To scourge these people, and revenge your wrongs.
For this night I'll betake me to my tent.

Tar. And we to ours; to morrow we'll renown
Our army with the spoil of this rich town.   *[exeunt*

SCENE V.

Enter PORSENNA *and* SECRETARY.

Por. Our secretary.

Sec. My lord!

Por. Command lights and torches in our tents.

Enter SOLDIERS *with torches.*

And let a guard engirt our safety round,
Whilst we debate of military business
Come, sit, and let's consult.

Enter SCÆVOLA, *disguised.*

Scæ. Horatius, famous for defending Rome,
But we have done nought worthy Scævola,
Nor of a Roman: I, in this disguise,
Have pass'd the army and the puissant guard
Of king Porsenna: this should be his tent;
And in good time, how fate direct my strength
Against a king, to free great Rome at length.
         [stabs the Secretary.

Sec. Oh! I am slain! treason! treason!

Por. Villain! what hast thou done?

Scæ. Why, slain the king.

Por. What king?

Scæ. Porsenna.

Por. Porsenna lives to see thee tortur'd
With plagues more dev'lish than the pains of hell.

Scæ. Oh, too rash Mutius, hast thou miss'd thy aim?
And thou base hand, that did'st direct my poniard
Against a peasant's breast, behold, thy error
Thus I will punish: I will give thee freely
Unto the fire, nor will I wear a limb,

          [puts his hand into the fire.

That with such rashness shall offend his lord.

Por. What will the madman do?

Scæ. Porsenna so,
Punish my hand thus, for not killing thee.
Three hundred noble lads besides myself
Have vow'd to all the gods that patron Rome,
Thy ruin for supporting tyranny:
And though I fail, expect yet every hour,
When some strange fate thy fortunes will devour.

Por. Stay, Roman! we admire thy constancy,
And scorn of fortune; go, return to Rome,
We give thee life, and say, the king Porsenna,
Whose life thou seek'st, is in this honorable;
Pass freely; guard him to the walls of Rome,
And were we not so much engag'd to Tarquin,
We would not lift a hand against that nation
That breeds such noble spirits.

Scæ. Well, I go,
And for revenge take life even of my foe.   *[exit.*

Por. Conduct him safely: what! three hundred gallants

Sworn to our death, and all resolv'd like him!
We must be provident, to-morrow's fortune
We'll prove for Tarquins, if they fail our hopes,
Peace shall be made with Rome; but first our secretary
Shall have his rites of funeral, then our shield
We must address next for to-morrow's field.   [*exit.*

SCENE VI.

Enter BRUTUS, HORATIUS, VALERIUS, COLLATINE, *and* LUCRETIUS,
marching.

Bru. By thee we are consul, and still govern Rome,
Which but for thee, had been despoil'd and ta'en,
Made a confused heap of men and stones,
Swimming in blood and slaughter; dear Horatius,
Thy noble picture shall be carv'd in brass,
And fix'd for thy perpetual memory
In our high Capitol.

    Hor. Great consul, thanks!
But leaving this, let's march out of the city,
And once more bid them battle on the plains.

    Val. This day my soul divines we shall live free
From all the furious Tarquins; but where's Scævola?
We see not him to-day.

Enter SCÆVOLA.

    Scæ. Here, lords, behold me handless, as you see.
The cause,—I miss'd Porsenna in his tent,
And in his stead kill'd but his secretary.
The 'mazed king, when he beheld me punish
My rash mistake, with loss of my right hand;

Unbegg'd, and almost scorn'd, he gave me life,
Which I had then refus'd, but in desire
To 'venge fair Lucrece' rape.
   Hor. Dear Scævola,
Thou hast exceeded us in our resolve;
But will the Tarquins give us present battle?
   Scæ. That may ye hear;   [*soft alarum*.
The skirmish is begun already 'twixt the horse.
   Luc. Then, noble consul, lead our main battle on!
   Bru. O Jove! this day balance our cause,
And let her innocent blood destroy
The heads of all the Tarquins! See, this day,
In her cause do we consecrate our lives,
And in defence of justice now march on;
I hear their martial music, be our shock
As terrible as are the meeting clouds
That break in thunder; yet our hopes are fair,
And this rough charge shall all our loss repair.
              [*exeunt; alarum, battle within*.

SCENE VII.

Enter PORSENNA *and* ARUNS.

   Por. Yet grow our lofty plumes unflagg'd with blood,
And yet sweet pleasure wantons in the air:
How goes the battle, Aruns?
   Aru. 'Tis even balanc'd;
I interchang'd with Brutus, hand to hand,
A dangerous encounter; both are wounded;
And had not the rude press divided us,
One had dropp'd down to earth.

Por. 'Twas bravely fought. I saw the king, your father, free his person from a thousand Romans that begirt his state, where flying arrows, thick as atoms, sung about his ears.

Aru. I hope a glorious day ; come, Tuscan king, let's on them !   [*alarum.*

Enter HORATIUS *and* VALERIUS.

Hor. Aruns, stay ; that sword that late did drink the consul's blood, must, with keen fang, tire upon my flesh, or this on thine.

Aru. It spar'd the consul's life
To end thy days in a more glorious strife.

Val. I stand against thee, Tuscan !

Por. I for thee !

Hor. Where e'er I find a Tarquin, he's for me !
            [*alarum, fight ; Aruns slain, Porsenna expulsed.*

Alarum—Enter TARQUIN *with an arrow in his breast,* TULLIA
    with him, pursued by COLLATINE, LUCRETIUS, *and* SCÆVOLA.

Tar. Fair Tullia, leave me ; save thy life by flight,
Since mine is desperate ; behold, I'm wounded
Even to the death : there stays within my tent
A winged jennet, mount his back and fly :
Live to revenge my death, since I must die.

Tul. Had I the heart to tread upon the bulk
Of my dead father, and to see him slaughter'd
Only for love of Tarquin and a crown ;
And shall I fear death more than loss of both ?
No, this is Tullia's fame, rather than fly
From Tarquin, 'mongst a thousand swords she'll die !

All. Hew them to pieces both!

Tar. My Tullia save,

And o'er my caitiff head those meteors wave.

Col. Let Tullia yield then!

Tul. Yield me, cuckold? no;

Mercy I scorn, let me the danger know!

Scæ. Upon them, then!

Val. Let's bring them to their fate,

And let them perish in the people's hate.

Tul. Fear not, I'll back thee, husband.

Tar. But for thee,

Sweet were the hand that this charg'd soul could free;

Life I despise, let noble Sextus stand

T'avenge our death; even till these vitals end,

Scorning my own, thy life will I defend!

Tul. And I'll, sweet Tarquin, to my power guard thine:

Come on, ye slaves, and make this earth divine!

      [*alarum; Tarquin and Tullia are slain*

   Alarum. Enter BRUTUS, *all bloody.*

Bru. Aruns, this crimson favour for thy sake,

I'll wear upon my forehead, mask'd with blood,

Till all the moisture in the Tarquins' veins

Be spilt upon the earth; and leave thy body

As dry as the parch'd summer, burnt and scorch'd

With the canicular stars.

Hor. Aruns lies dead,

By this bright sword that tower'd above his head!

Col. And see, great consul,

Where the pride of Rome lies sunk and fallen.

Val. Beside him lies the queen mangled and hewn
Amongst the Roman soldiers.

Hor. Lift up their slaughter'd bodies; help to rear
Them 'gainst this hill in view of all the camp.
This sight will be a terror to the foe,
And make them yield or fly.

Bru. But where's the ravisher,
Injurious Sextus, that we see not him?   [*short alarum.*

Enter SEXTUS.

Sex. Through broken spears, crack'd swords, unbowel'd
       steeds,
Flaw'd armours, mangl'd limbs, and batter'd casques,
Knee-deep in blood, I've pierc'd the Roman host
To be my father's rescue.

Hor. 'Tis too late;
His mounting pride's sunk in the people's hate.

Sex. My father, mother, brother! fortune, now
I do defy thee! I expose myself
To horrid danger; safety I despise:
I dare the worst of peril, I am bound
On till this pile of flesh be all one wound.

Val. Begirt him, lords! this is the ravisher;
There's no revenge for Lucrece till he fall.

Luc. Cease, Sextus, then.

Sex. Sextus defies you all!
Yet, will you give me language ere I die?

Bru. Say on.

Sex. 'Tis not for mercy, for I scorn that life
That's given by any; and the more to add

To your immense unmeasurable hate,
I was the spur unto my father's pride.
'Twas I that aw'd the princes of the land,
That made thee, Brutus, mad; these discontent;
I ravish'd the chaste Lucrece; Sextus I,
Thy daughter, and thy wife; Brutus, thy cousin,
Alli'd indeed to all; 'twas for my rape,
Her constant hand ripp'd up her innocent breast;
'Twas Sextus did all this!

    Col. Which I'll revenge!

    Hor. Leave that to me.

    Luc. Old as I am, I'll do't!

    Scæ. I have one hand left yet,
Of strength enough to kill a ravisher.

    Sex. Come all at once, aye, all!
Yet hear me, Brutus, thou art honourable,
And my words tend to thee: my father dy'd
By many hands; what's he 'mongst you can challenge
The least, aye, smallest honour in his death?
If I be kill'd among this hostile throng,
The poorest snaky soldier well may claim
As much renown in noble Sextus' death,
As Brutus, thou, or thou, Horatius:
I am to die, and more than die I cannot:
Rob not yourselves of honour in my death.
When the two mightiest spirits of Greece and Troy
Tugg'd for the mast'ry, Hector and Achilles;
Had puissant Hector, by Achilles' hand,
Dy'd in single monomachy, Achilles
Had been the worthy; but being slain by odds,

The poorest Myrmidon had as much honour
As faint Achilles in the Trojan's death.

   Bru. Had'st thou not done a deed so execrable
That gods and men abhor, I'd love thee, Sextus,
And hug thee for this challenge breath'd so freely:
Behold, I stand for Rome as general;
Thou of the Tarquins dost alone survive,
The head of all these garboils, the chief actor
Of that black sin, which we chastise by arms.
Brave Romans, with your bright swords be our lists,
And ring us in; none dare t'offend the prince
By the least touch, lest he incur our wrath;
This honour do your consul, that his hand
May punish this arch-mischief; that the times
Succeeding may of Brutus thus much tell,
By him pride, lust, and all the Tarquins fell.

   Sex. To ravish Lucrece, cuckold Collatine,
And spill the chastest blood that ever ran
In any matron's veins, repents me not
So much as to have wrong'd a gentleman
So noble as the consul in this strife.
Brutus, be bold, thou fight'st with one scorns life.

   Bru. And thou with one, that less than his renown,
Prizeth his blood or Rome's imperial crown.

      [*alarum: a fierce fight, with sword and target; they*
                     pause and breathe.

   Bru. Sextus, stand fair, much honour shall I win,
To revenge Lucrece, and chastise thy sin.

   Sex. I repent nothing, may I live or die;
Though my blood fall, my spirit shall mount on high.

[Alarum :—fight with single swords, and being deadly wounded and panting for breath, making a stroke at each other with their gauntlets, they fall.

Hor. Both slain ! Oh, noble Brutus, this thy fame
To after ages shall survive ; thy body
Shall have a fair and gorgeous sepulchre :
For whom the matrons shall in funeral black
Mourn twelve sad moons ; thou that first govern'd Rome,
And sway'd the people by a consul's name.
These bodies of the Tarquins we'll commit
Unto the funeral pile : you, Collatine,
Shall succeed Brutus in the consul's place,
Whom with this laurel wreath we here create.

       [crowns him with laurel.

Such is the people's voice, accept it then.

Col. We do, and may our pow'r so just appear,
Rome may have peace, both with our love and fear.
But soft ! what march is this ?

   Flourish. Enter PORSENNA *and* SOLDIERS.

Por. The Tuscan king seeing the Tarquins slain,
Thus arm'd and battl'd, offers peace to Rome ;
To confirm which, we'll give you present hostage ;
If you deny, we'll stand upon our guard,
And by the force of arms, maintain our own.

Val. After so much effusion and large waste
Of Roman blood, the name of peace is welcome :
Since of the Tarquins none remain in Rome,
And Lucrece' rape is now reveng'd at full,

'Twere good to entertain Porsenna's league.

   Col. Porsenna we embrace, whose royal presence
Shall grace the consul to the funeral pile.

     March on to Rome! Jove be our guard and guide!

     That hath, in us, veng'd rape, and punish'd pride!

                          [exeunt.

THE END.

"Yesterday's Treasures for Today's Readers"

Titles by Benediction Classics available from Amazon.co.uk

Religio Medici, Hydriotaphia, Letter to a Friend, Thomas Browne

Pseudodoxia Epidemica: Or, Enquiries into Commonly Presumed Truths, Thomas Browne

The Maid's Tragedy, Beaumont and Fletcher

The Custom of the Country, Beaumont and Fletcher

Philaster Or Love Lies a Bleeding, Beaumont and Fletcher

A Treatise of Fishing with an Angle,   Dame Juliana Berners.

Pamphilia to Amphilanthus, Lady Mary Wroth

The Compleat Angler, Izaak Walton

The Magnetic Lady, Ben Jonson

Every Man Out of His Humour, Ben Jonson

The Masque of Blacknesse. The Masque of Beauty,. Ben Jonson

The Life of St. Thomas More, William Roper

Pendennis, William Makepeace Thackeray

Salmacis and Hermaphroditus attributed to Francis Beaumont

Friar Bacon and Friar Bungay Robert Greene

Holy Wisdom, Augustine Baker

The Jew of Malta and the Massacre at Paris, Christopher Marlowe

Tamburlaine the Great, Parts 1 & 2 AND Massacre at Paris, Christopher Marlowe

All Ovids Elegies, Lucans First Booke, Dido Queene of Carthage, Hero and Leander, Christopher Marlowe

The Titan, Theodore Dreiser

Scapegoats of the Empire: The true story of the Bushveldt Carbineers, George Witton

All Hallows' Eve, Charles Williams

My Apprenticeship: Volumes I and II, Beatrice Webb

Last and First Men / Star Maker, Olaf Stapledon

Last and First Men, Olaf Stapledon

Darkness and the Light, Olaf Stapledon

The Worst Journey in the World, Apsley Cherry-Garrard

The Schoole of Abuse, Containing a Pleasaunt Invective Against Poets, Pipers, Plaiers, Iesters and Such Like Catepillers of the Commonwelth, Stephen Gosson

Russia in the Shadows, H. G. Wells

Wild Swans at Coole, W. B. Yeats

A hundreth good pointes of husbandrie, Thomas Tusser

The Collected Works of Nathanael West: "The Day of the Locust", "The Dream Life of Balso Snell", "Miss Lonelyhearts", "A Cool Million", Nathanael West

Miss Lonelyhearts & The Day of the Locust, Nathaniel West

The Worst Journey in the World, Apsley Cherry-Garrard

Scott's Last Expedition, V1, R. F. Scott

The Dream of Gerontius, John Henry Newman

The Brother of Daphne, Dornford Yates

The Poetry of Architecture: Or the Architecture of the Nations of Europe Considered in Its Association with Natural Scenery and National Character, John Ruskin

The Downfall of Robert Earl of Huntington, Anthony Munday

Clayhanger, Arnold Bennett

South: The Story of Shackleton's Last Expedition 1914-1917, Sir Ernest Shackketon

Greene's Groatsworth of Wit: Bought With a Million of Repentance, Robert Greene

Beau Sabreur, Percival Christopher Wren

The Hekatompathia, or Passionate Centurie of Love, Thomas Watson

The Art of Rhetoric, Thomas Wilson

Stepping Heavenward, Elizabeth Prentiss

Barker's Delight, or The Art of Angling, Thomas Barker
The Napoleon of Notting Hill, G.K. Chesterton

The Douay-Rheims Bible (The Challoner Revision)

Endimion - The Man in the Moone, John Lyly

Gallathea and Midas, John Lyly,

Manners, Custom and Dress During the Middle Ages and During the Renaissance Period, Paul Lacroix

Obedience of a Christian Man, William Tyndale

St. Patrick for Ireland, James Shirley

The Wrongs of Woman; Or Maria/Memoirs of the Author of a Vindication of the Rights of Woman, Mary Wollstonecraft and William Godwin

De Adhaerendo Deo. Of Cleaving to God, Albertus Magnus

Obedience of a Christian Man, William Tyndale

A Trick to Catch the Old One, Thomas Middleton

The Princely Pleasures at Kenelworth Castle, George Gascoigne

The Fair Maid of the West. Part I and Part II. Thomas Heywood

Proserpina, Volume I and Volume II. Studies of Wayside Flowers, John Ruskin

The Endeavour Journal of Sir Joseph Banks. Sir Joseph Banks

Christ Legends: And Other Stories, Selma Lagerlof; (trans. Velma Swanston Howard)

Chamber Music, James Joyce

Blurt, Master Constable, Thomas Middleton, Thomas Dekker

Since Yesterday, Frederick Lewis Allen

The Scholemaster: Or, Plaine and Perfite Way of Teachyng Children the Latin Tong , Roger Ascham

The Wonderful Year, 1603, Thomas Dekker

Waverley, Sir Walter Scott

Guy Mannering, Sir Walter Scott

Old Mortality, Sir Walter Scott

The Knight of Malta, John Fletcher

Space Prison, Tom Godwin

The Home of the Blizzard Being the Story of the Australasian Antarctic Expedition, 1911-1914, Douglas Mawson

Wild-goose Chase , John Fletcher

If You Know Not Me, You Know Nobody. Part I and Part II, Thomas Heywood

The Ragged Trousered Philanthropists, Robert Tressell

The Greater Trumps, Charles Williams

The Island of Sheep, John Buchan

Eyes of the Woods, Joseph Altsheler

The Club of Queer Trades, G. K. Chesterton

The Financier, Theodore Dreiser

Something of Myself, Rudyard Kipling

Law of Freedom in a Platform, or True Magistracy Restored, Gerrard Winstanley

Damon and Pithias, Richard Edwards

Dido Queen of Carthage: And, The Massacre at Paris, Christopher Marlowe

Cocoa and Chocolate: Their History from Plantation to Consumer, Arthur Knapp

Lady of Pleasure, James Shirley

The South Pole: An account of the Norwegian Antarctic expedition in the "Fram," 1910-12. Volume 1 and Volume 2, Roald Amundsen

and many others…

Tell us what you would love to see in print again, at affordable prices!
Email: **benedictionbooks@btinternet.com**